the early earth

the early earth

john c. whitcomb

baker book house   grand rapids, michigan

Copyright © 1972 by
Baker Book House Company

ISBN: 0-8010-9524-7

Thirteenth printing, February 1985

Picture credits

Cover, 15, 19, 35, 39, 45, 49, 53, 61, 67, 75, 79, 83, 85, 89, 93, 101,
113, 119, 133 — H. Armstrong Roberts
57 — Underwood and Underwood
71 — The American Museum of Natural History

Printed in the United States of America

To

my father

Col. John Clement Whitcomb (Ret.)

In grateful and loving

appreciation

acknowledgments

The writer hereby expresses his deep appreciation to Dr. Henry M. Morris, for many years the Head of the Department of Civil Engineering at Virginia Polytechnic Institute and now Director of the Creation Science Research Center, San Diego, California. For fifteen years he has generously shared of his rich experience in the Word of God and in the natural sciences. Though separated by half a continent in our professional labors, it has been a close association in the joyous task of exploring God's universe in the light of His written revelation. Dr. Morris has read the manuscript in its original form and has written the Foreword.

Appreciation is also expressed to the Reformed Fellowship, Inc., Grand Rapids, Michigan, for sponsoring a series of lectures on "Creation According to God's Word" and publishing them in booklet form in 1966. Chapter 1, chapter 3, and chapter 4 of the present work are adaptations of those lectures.

Chapter 2 is a revision of an article which appeared in the Creation Research Society Quarterly of September, 1967, and is being used by the kind permission of the Editor, Dr. George F. Howe.

Portions of chapter 5 have appeared previously in the 1965 Annual and the September, 1971, Quarterly of the Creation Research Society.

Mr. Robert Ibach, Jr., Library Assistant for Grace Theological Seminary and Teaching Assistant in Old Testament and Archaeology, has graciously consented to proofread the entire manuscript and to prepare the Bibliography.

foreword

To interpret the Bible literally is simply to take God at His Word. This is the high road of Biblical exposition which readers have learned to anticipate in anything written by John Whitcomb, and the studies in this book are outstanding examples of such God-honoring exposition.

Any study by Dr. Whitcomb dealing with the Genesis record is certain to be authoritative and relevant. The chapters in this small book have already been widely read and used to strengthen the confidence of many people in the integrity of God's Word. Even the early chapters of Genesis should be recognized as completely historical and scientifically accurate, and this is the position demonstrated and expounded in these pages.

I am glad to endorse this book, not only because of the high scholarship and careful exegesis which I know always characterize the writings of Dr. Whitcomb, but also because our many years of close friendship have enabled me to know him as humble and gracious, a Spirit-filled servant of the Lord Jesus Christ.

I surely hope and believe that these important studies, now assembled for the first time in book form, will enjoy a much wider ministry in this way. They are certainly needed in this day of widespread compromise and retreat and will be commended "by the word of truth, by the power of God" (II Cor. 6:7).

Henry M. Morris

preface

Life on the planet Earth reveals the clear signs of its coming extinction. The drift of quality and order is not upward, but downward. Even as the force of gravity inevitably brings each flying arrow to the ground, so all of nature seems to be programmed to weaken, kill, and disintegrate the fantastically complex and delicately beautiful life forms that once filled the earth in vast abundance.

In spite of the enormous influence of Darwin's theories in modern education, many specialists in the natural sciences are becoming convinced that nature can neither create nor improve non-living and living things. The sun dissipates its vast nuclear energy at the stupendous expense of four million tons of its mass per second. And this loss can never be regained! High-level energy systems are inevitably reduced to low-level energy systems, and thus the spectre of a universal "heat-death" darkens the horizon.

Living systems are similarly trapped in this universal slide toward disorder. Plants, animals, and human beings all lose their original genetic powers through the accumulation of harmful mutations and through the downward gradient of genetic depletion. In opposition to the Neo-Darwinian concept of inevitable progress, the Bible agrees with the observed facts of progressive disorder: "The earth and the heavens . . . shall perish, but thou shalt endure; yea, all of them shall wax old like a garment; as a vesture shalt thou change them, and they shall be changed: but thou art the same, and thy years shall have no end" (Ps. 102:25-27).

However, strange as it may seem, this very fact of universal deterioration (confirmed and interpreted by God's written revelation) points to man's only true hope of immortality! For if the universe has been evolving into higher and higher forms, as Neo-Darwinists believe, then the Biblical world-view and God's firm promise of eternal salvation to those who believe Him would be hopelessly discredited.

On the other hand, the inexorable grip of the second law of thermodynamics (which states that disorder in a closed system increases with time) forces us to the conclusion that the earth was once more organized and integrated and beautiful than it is now. And this in turn points to an infinite and personal God who alone could have infused order and high-level energy into the universe at the beginning.

Christians believe that this great Creator has condescended to tell us what the early earth was really like and how it was brought into being. This record has been preserved for us in that unparalleled account of ultimate origins, the Book of Genesis. What this Book tells us about the condition of the earth at the dawn of its existence is of vast importance. For upon this question hinges not only the nature and dignity of man, but also his destiny. The Bible informs us that the perfection of the early earth was an appropriate reflection of man's original fellowship with his Creator. Unfallen man exercised *full dominion* over the earth and its living creatures (Gen. 1:26-28). God put *all things* under his feet and crowned him with glory and honor (Ps. 8:5-8; Heb. 2:5-8). But man rebelled against his gracious Creator and the earth was transformed into its present pattern of frustration, suffering, and death. "For by one man sin entered into the world, and death by sin. . . . For the creation was made subject to vanity, not willingly but by reason of Him who hath subjected the same. . . . For we know that the whole creation groaneth and travaileth in pain together until now" (Rom. 5:12; 8:20-22).

But for those among men who repent of sin and turn back to God in obedient faith, the prospect of the future is bright beyond description. After describing the removal of the "reign of tooth and claw" that has characterized the animal kingdom since the fall of man, the prophet Isaiah states that "they shall not hurt nor destroy in all my holy mountain; for the earth shall be full of the knowledge of the Lord, as the waters cover the sea" (Isa. 11:9). This can only be appreciated in the light of Biblical revelation concerning the early earth (Gen. 1:29-31).

In identical fashion, the Apostle Peter assured the nation of Israel that if they repented of their rejection of Christ, "times of refreshing shall come from the presence of the Lord; and he shall send Jesus Christ, who before was preached unto you, whom the heaven must receive until the times of restitution of all things, which God hath spoken by the mouth of his holy prophets since the age began" (Acts 3:19-21). Since *restitution* (Gk. *apokatastasis*) means "restoration to a former state," it is obvious that the original perfections of the earth will once again be experienced by those who take God at His Word.

As we see the present earth deteriorating before our very eyes, may this brief study of the early earth arouse within the heart of each reader a deep desire to discover and experience God's announced remedy for the impending crisis: genuine faith in the Lord Jesus Christ as the only Saviour of mankind.

THE PLANET EARTH

The early earth, as it would be viewed from outer space before the great Flood, was quite different from its present appearance. In the first place, it would have been even more colorful than it is now (see cover picture), for there would have been no cloud canopy to obscure the brilliant blue oceans. Secondly, there would have been no white polar caps or reddish-brown desert regions, for thick green vegetation covered almost all of the land areas, even in polar regions (thick coal deposits have been recently discovered in the mountains of Antarctica). And thirdly, the continents were probably quite different in shape and location. Some regions that are now high above sea level were once under the oceans. Many Bible scholars believe that there was only one great land mass surrounded by seas before the Flood, because two each of all kinds of air-breathing animals walked to Noah's Ark (Gen. 6:20, 7:9). It is also possible, how-ever, that if there were more than one continent, representatives of all the kinds of animals were living on each continent. The idea that continents have "drifted" into their present locations faces serious geophysical ob-jections and is not really supported by Scripture (Gen. 10:25 must refer to the dividing of nations after the Tower of Babel judgment; cf. 10:5, 20, 32).

contents

1

the nature
of biblical creation

Creation Was Supernatural

In forthright opposition to all efforts to explain the origin of the world in terms of purely natural processes, the Bible states that *God* created all things *supernaturally*. In other words, the world came into being in a way that was entirely different from anything that may be observed in the present universe. Today, absolutely nothing can be created directly apart from preexistent materials, and scientists express this basic truth in terms of the first law of thermodynamics. Genuine creation is no longer being accomplished, as the Bible clearly states (Gen. 2:1-3). God's work of *preservation* keeps the universe in existence (Heb. 1:3), and His work of *providence* directs the universe towards glorious goals (Col. 1:20), but His work of *creation,* as far as the present universe is concerned, has been completed.

Thus, when God created "the heavens, the earth, the sea, and all that in them is" (Exod. 20:11; 31:17), He did so without the use of any preexistent materials whatsoever. In one moment there was no physical substance anywhere; in the next moment the heavens and the earth sprang into existence. Theologians have called this *creatio ex nihilo* (creation out of nothing), and this expression is helpful if we understand it to mean that *physical* entities were created out of the nonphysical resources of God's omnipotence. Technically, the expression is applicable only to the creation of inorganic substances, for God did employ previously created inorganic materials in forming the bodies of living things. Nevertheless, even in this case, as we shall see, creation was strictly supernatural.

The fact that creation was supernatural means, among other things, that it can be grasped by the human mind only through the channel of *special revelation*. God alone can tell us how the world began, because no man was there to see it being created, and even if a human observer had been present, he could not have understood fully what he saw apart from God's own interpretation.

"Gird up now thy loins like a man," said God to Job, "for I will demand of thee, and answer thou me. Where wast thou when I laid the foundations of the earth? Declare, if thou hast understanding" (Job 38:3-4).

However, our difficulty in grasping the doctrine of creation is not due so much to the fact that we are *finite* as to the fact that we are *sinful*. "The natural man receiveth not the things of the Spirit of God: for they are foolishness unto him: neither can he know them, because they are spiritually discerned" (I Cor. 2:14). There are few doctrines of the Bible that seem more foolish to the natural man than that of supernatural creation, for such events are not happening today. But creation is at the same time most definitely one of the supremely important "things of the Spirit of God," for without it the Scriptures and Christianity would fall to pieces. Remove this doctrine, and the entire superstructure collapses.

It is therefore exceedingly important that we approach the first chapters of Genesis in the light that God Himself provides through the entire testimony of Scripture. Even as God commanded Moses to put off his shoes because the place whereon he stood was holy ground, so likewise we must set aside our concepts of what could or could not have happened, and stand in God's presence, ready to hear and to believe what He has chosen to tell us about creation.

Such unconditional submission to the authority of the Word of God is not, of course, the mood of our day, even among Christians. Paul warned that "the time would come when they will not endure sound doctrine; but after their own lusts shall they heap to themselves teachers, having itching ears; and they shall turn away their ears from the truth, and shall be turned unto fables" (II Tim. 4:3-4). One such fable, we believe, is that God did not create the world supernaturally, but employed natural processes, by His providence, through vast periods of time. It is a fable, not simply because it contradicts Scripture, but because it contradicts the actual facts of science.

In recent years, remarkable testimony has been forthcoming from the pens of highly respected scientists to the effect that the evolution concept, in its broader aspect, rests upon a vanishing foundation. Dr. G. A. Kerkut of the Department of Physiology and Biochemistry at the University of Southampton, for example, notes that evolutionists often write as though they "have had their views by some sort of revelation." In spite of "many gaps and failures" in their system, it is "taken on trust" by a "blind acceptance" and a "closing of the eyes" to many important facts, thus revealing an "arrogant" rather than truly scientific spirit.[1] Attempts to bridge the gap between invertebrates and vertebrates for example, have resulted in "science fiction" rather than discovery,[2] and the possibility that life first began spontaneously is a "matter of faith on the part of the biologist."[3]

In his introduction to Darwin's *Origin of Species* in the *Everyman Library,* Dr. W. R. Thompson points out that "modern Darwinian palaeontologists are obliged, just like their predecessors and like Darwin, to water down the facts with subsidiary hypotheses, which, however plausible, are in the nature of things unverifiable . . . and the reader is left with the feeling that if the data do not support the theory they really ought to. . . . This situation, where scientific men rally to the defence of a doctrine they are unable to define scientifically, much less demonstrate with scientific rigour, attempting to maintain its credit with the public by the suppression of criticism and the elimination of difficulties, is abnormal and undesirable in science."[4]

Several years ago, Dr. Richard B. Goldschmidt, a leading geneticist, stated that "the incessant repetition of this unproved claim (of micromutational evolution), glossing

---

[1]*Implications of Evolution* (New York: Pergamon Press, 1960), pp. 154, 155.

[2]Ibid., p. 153.

[3]Ibid., p. 150.

[4]Reprinted in *Journal of the American Scientific Affiliation,* March 1960, pp. 7, 8.

lightly over the difficulties, and the assumption of an arrogant attitude toward those who are not so easily swayed by fashions of science, are considered to afford scientific proof of the doctrine."[5] The late Dr. J. J. Duyvene De Wit of the Department of Zoology at the University of the Orange Free State, has pointed out that the "dualistic split" between scientific *knowledge* (pertaining to discontinuity between kinds of living things) and suprascientific *faith* (in evolutionary continuity) amounts to "a rift in the consciousness of the biologist personally."[6]

The general theory of evolution, therefore, as an antitheistic faith, has been increasingly contradicted by the facts of science during the past century. Christians who accept the clear testimony of Scripture concerning the supernatural character of original creation are confident that the true facts of science, though frequently suppressed and misinterpreted by evolutionists, will ultimately be found to harmonize with the Bible.

Creation Was Sudden

An important aspect of the supernaturalism of the original creation was its *suddenness*. Creation was not only *ex nihilo* (in reference especially to the earth, the sun, the moon, and the stars), but it was also, in the very nature of the case, instantaneous. The evolutionary concept of a gradual buildup of heavier and heavier elements throughout cosmic history (for example, in Gamow's "Big-Bang Theory") is clearly excluded by Scripture.

In the first place, note the emphasis on the immediate effect of God's creative word in Psalm 33:6, 9 — "By the word of the Lord were the heavens made; and all the host of them by the breath of His mouth . . . for He spake, and it was done; he commanded, and it stood fast." There is certainly no thought here of delay, or a trial-and-error

---

[5]"Evolution, As Viewed by One Geneticist," *American Scientist,* January 1952, p. 94.

[6]*A New Critique of the Transformist Principle in Evolutionary Biology* (Kampen, Neth.: Kok, 1965), p. 43.

process, or a gradual, step-by-step fulfillment. In fact, it is quite impossible to imagine a time interval in the transition from nonexistence to existence! "And God said, Let there be light: and there was light" (Gen. 1:3). At one moment there was no light; the next moment there was! Analogous to this is the absolute supernaturalism, perfection, and suddenness of God's work of regeneration in the sinful heart of man: "For God, who commanded the light to shine out of darkness, hath shined in our hearts, to give the light of the knowledge of the glory of God in the face of Jesus Christ" (II Cor. 4:6). The idea of *sudden appearance* thus completely saturates the entire creation account, and there is really no alternative to this from a logical standpoint when the first and second laws of thermodynamics are taken into account.

When God created *living things,* He chose to use previously created inorganic substances for the bodies of these creatures. Thus, He commanded the waters to bring forth marine creatures and birds on the fifth day. But the water, of itself, contributed nothing to the complex physical structure and life principle of these animals, just as the water Jesus used at Cana of Galilee could never have turned into wine, even if it vibrated with evolutionary anticipation in those stone jars for millions of years! In both cases, complex entities appeared suddenly, even though built upon preexistent lifeless materials. The earth was commanded by God to bring forth trees, but this does not imply a gradual growth process any more than God's use of the same earth to bring forth the full-grown body of a man at a later time in creation week. Many have erred seriously at this point, as we shall explain in chapter 4.

One writer has characterized this view as "deistic," "irruptive," "ictic," and dangerously close to the theology of the pagan Ephesians who believed that the image of Diana had hurtled upon them out of heaven.[7] Typical of this type of creationism, we are told, is the modern funda-

---

[7]Leonard Verduin, "Man, a Created Being: What of an Animal Ancestry?" *Christianity Today,* May 21, 1965, p. 10.

mentalist movement which "is natively happy in the presence of the ictic and natively ill at ease in the presence of the processive" and thus assigns a large place "to the idea of the Second Coming, looked upon as in no sense the fruition of the historic process but as something brought about simply and solely by the interrupting voice of God."[8] The validity of this type of objection rests, of course, upon the validity of the assumption that general evolution is true, that miracles can be explained usually in terms of process, and that God created the world "with the prodigal disregard for the passing of time that marks the hand of him who fashions a work of art."[9]

This leads us to our second consideration, the analogy of Christ's miraculous works during His earthly ministry. Since the New Testament makes it clear that Christ, the Son of God, was the original Creator of the world (John 1:3, Col. 1:16, Heb. 1:2), and that the works He performed during His brief earthly ministry were intended to reveal His true nature and glory (John 1:14; 2:11; 20:31), it is deeply instructive to note that these works involved *sudden* transformations in nature and in human bodies. At His word, a storm suddenly ceased, a fig tree suddenly withered, a man born blind suddenly has his sight restored, a dead man suddenly stood at the entrance of his tomb. Of the vast number of miracles performed by Christ, the only recorded exception to instantaneous cures is that of the blind man whose sight was restored in two stages, each stage, however, being instantaneous (Mark 8:25). Such miracles were undeniable signs of supernaturalism in our Lord's public claim to Messiahship, and we may be sure that if, in His healing of the sick and crippled and blind, He had exhibited "the prodigal disregard for the passing of time that marks the hand of him who fashions a work of art," no one would have paid any attention to His claims!

In the third place, the fact that God's work of creation was completed in six literal days clearly demonstrates that

[8]Ibid., p. 11.
[9]Ibid., p. 10.

the work of each day was sudden. In view of the wide-spread resistance to this concept in some Christian circles today, it is surprising how many strong Biblical arguments are available in its support, if the time-honored, historical-grammatical system of Biblical hermeneutics be accepted. *First,* the use of a numerical adjective with the word *day* in Genesis 1 limits it to a normal day. It is true that the word *day* is used in two or even in three different senses in the creation narrative (of a twelve-hour period of day-light in 1:5, 14, 16, 18; of a twenty-four-hour day in the rest of the chapter; and of the entire creation week in 2:4, though this verse may refer only to the first day of crea-tion), but in each case the context shows what sense is to be understood. In historical narratives the numerical adjective *always* limits the word to a twenty-four-hour pe-riod (cf. Num. 7 for a remarkable parallel).

Second, the qualifying phrase, "there was evening and there was morning," attached to each of these days points to a twenty-four-hour day-night cycle. The same phrase appears in Daniel 8:26 (cf. 8:14 ASV), and orthodox interpreters have always understood this as referring to twenty-three hundred literal days. *Third,* a creation week of six indefinite periods of time would hardly serve as a valid and meaningful pattern for man's cycle of work and rest, as explained by God in the fourth commandment (Exod. 20:11, 31:17). It is certainly true that God could have created the world in six seconds, but the fourth commandment suggests that He chose to do so in six days to serve as a pattern for man's work and rest periods. *Fourth,* we may assume that the first three days of creation were the same length as the last three in reference to which God set lights in the heavens "for seasons, and for days, and for years" (1:14), because exactly the same de-scriptive phrases are used of each group of three days. The fact that the sun was not created until the fourth day does not make the first three days indefinite periods of time, for on the first day God created a localized light source in the heaven in reference to which the rotating earth passed through the same night-day cycle.

In an essay entitled "The Creation of Matter, Life, and Man," Dr. Addison H. Leitch has sought to set aside the literal-day interpretation on the basis that "it would be easy for an Eskimo to argue for a six-month day instead of a twenty-four hour day."[10] However, it would seem that even Eskimos realize from an observation of the stars and the phases of sunlight that a day lasts about twenty-four hours; and even if they didn't know this, it still would not change the normal meaning of "day" throughout the Bible.

Dr. Leitch also claims that "other passages of Scripture tell us that 'a day in God's sight is as a thousand years.' "[11] But neither Psalm 90:4 nor II Peter 3:8 lend support to the day-age theory. The latter verse, for example, does not say that God's days last a thousand years, but that "one day is with the Lord *as* a thousand years." In other words, God is above the limitations of time in the sense that He can accomplish in *one literal day* what nature or man could not accomplish in a vast period of time, if ever. Note that one day is *"as* a thousand years," not *"is* a thousand years," with God. If "one day" in this verse means a long period of time, then we would end up with the following absurdity: "a long period of time is with the Lord as a thousand years." Instead of this, the verse reveals how much God can actually accomplish in a literal day of twenty-four hours.

Yet another objection to the literal-day interpretation is that the seventh day did not end in twenty-four hours, for God still rests from His work of creation. However, Exodus 20:10-11 makes it clear that Israel was to observe a twenty-four-hour Sabbath, and God's sabbath was a pattern for this. Furthermore, Adam and Eve must have lived through the entire seventh day before God drove them out of the garden. Surely God would not have cursed the

---

[10]Fifth in a series of essays published by *Christianity Today*, September 16, 1966, p. 10.
[11]Ibid.

earth during the seventh day which He blessed and sanctified!

In conclusion, we may talk about "processes" during creation week if we wish to do so; but it must be understood that these were supernatural processes which occurred within very short periods of time, like the miracles of the Lord Jesus Christ. It is quite obvious, however, that this is not at all what theistic evolutionists mean when they refer to "creative process." Attempts have indeed been made to interpret creation week in terms of the normal workings of providence by an appeal to Genesis 2: 5,[12] but Edward J. Young has shown that this appeal is not valid, and that Genesis 2:1-3 draws a sharp line of demarcation between "special, divine, creative fiats" and God's normal work of providence.[13] To blur the distinction between creation and providence would be as disastrous as to put the supernatural conception of the Lord Jesus Christ on the same level as His natural birth. God, after all, does have the power to work miracles.

Creation Involved a Superficial Appearance of History

The supernaturalism and suddenness of creation provide a necessary background for the concept of creation with a superficial appearance of history or age. Few doctrines of Scripture have met with such misrepresentation and ridicule as this, not only by secular writers but also by some who claim to be evangelical Christians. At the same time, however, few doctrines are quite as far-reaching in their theological significance, and that for at least two reasons.

In the first place, if this doctrine were not true, there could have been no original creation by God at all. Dr. Henry M. Morris has made this point quite clear: "If God actually created anything at all, even the simplest atoms,

---

[12]M. G. Kline, "Because It Had Not Rained," *Westminster Theological Journal,* May, 1958, pp. 146-57.

[13]*Studies in Genesis One* (Nutley, N. J.: Presbyterian and Reformed Pub. Co., 1964), pp. 58-65.

those atoms or other creations would necessarily have an appearance of *some* age. There could be no *genuine* creation of any kind, without an initial appearance of age inherent in it. It would still be possible to interpret the newly-created matter in terms of some kind of previous evolutionary history. And if God could create atomic stuff with an appearance of age — *in other words, if God exists!* — then there is no reason why He could not, in full conformity with His character of truth, create a whole universe full-grown."[14]

In the second place, if the doctrine of creation with appearance of history is erroneous, then most of the recorded miracles of the Lord Jesus Christ could not have occurred. One evening on a mountainside near the Sea of Galilee, five thousand men and their families ate loaves and fishes that were created with an appearance of age. Here were tens of thousands of barley loaves composed of grains that had neither been harvested from fields nor baked in ovens! And here were at least ten thousand fishes that had never hatched from eggs or been caught in nets or been dried in the sun!

An equally clear example of this is recorded in the second chapter of John. When Christ began His public ministry on earth, the very first miracle He performed was intended to "manifest his glory" (John 2:11) as the Creator of the world (John 1:3, 14). How did He accomplish this? By instantly transforming about 150 gallons of water into delicious wine. Now wine is the end product of a long series of complex natural processes involving the drawing of water from the soil into the fruit of the grapevine, and the gradual transforming of this water into the juice of grapes. Even then, the ripened grapes must be picked, the juice squeezed out and the sediments allowed to settle down. But Jesus, the Lord of Creation, bypassed

---

[14]John C. Whitcomb, Jr. and Henry M. Morris, *The Genesis Flood* (Nutley, N. J.: Presbyterian and Reformed Pub. Co., 1961), p. 238.

all these natural and human processes and created the end product with an appearance of history.

Now it is instructive to note that the ruler of the feast, who "knew not whence it was," naturally assumed that this "good wine" had been somewhere "kept . . . until now" (2:10). This was a natural conclusion, of course, for neither he nor anyone else in the world had ever considered the possibility of wine coming directly from water. It *must,* therefore, have had a history of natural development. But he was mistaken. He did not know about the supernatural powers of Christ, the Creator God. If I understand the Scriptures correctly at this point, this is the underlying reason for *all* denials of supernatural creation. When contemplating the created works of the Lord Jesus Christ, whether it be sun, moon, earth, oceans, plants, animals, or human beings, the natural man, like the ruler of the feast, simply assumes that they have all been "kept" somewhere "until now," having passed through complex natural processes, from simple primitive forms, through vast periods of time.

It is not difficult to see how this principle applies also to every great miracle of healing performed by our Lord. The ninth chapter of John tells of a man born blind to whom Jesus gave perfect vision. The rulers of Israel refused to believe that the man brought before them could have had *a past history of congenital blindness* — until they consulted his parents. Their perplexity is understandable. As the healed man himself expressed it, "since the world began was it not heard that any man opened the eyes of one that was born blind" (9:32). In a moment, Jesus created the appearance of a man born with normal eyesight.

In like manner, Jesus created in Lazarus of Bethany the appearance of a man who had not yet died. Who, in his "right mind," would have imagined that the recent history of this man sitting at a table in Bethany (John 12:2) included four days of decomposition in a tomb? Every instance, therefore, of supernatural, sudden, and perfect healings of sick, crippled, or dead people involved the creation of the appearance of an immediately previous condition of health and strength that had not existed. Every priest who was called upon to examine the lepers whom Jesus cleansed must have pondered this question (cf. Matt. 8:4).

Modern critics of this doctrine frequently identify Biblical creationism with the extreme views of Philip Henry Gosse (1810-1888), who wrote a book entitled *Omphalos: An Attempt to Untie the Geological Knot.*[15] Gosse not only believed that Adam was created with a navel (hence the name of the book, from the Greek word for navel), but also that all conceivable geologic formations, including fossiliferous strata, were created *in situ.*[16]

G. J. Renier comments that "if Philip Gosse is right, a fundamentalist Christian can be a scientist, but it is impossible for him to be an historian."[17] With this judgment we are in general agreement, for Gosse's concept of the creation of fossils actually involves a *denial of Biblical history,* especially the history of the Edenic Curse with the introduction of physical death as an effect of man's sin, and the great Flood with its unique capacity for the burial of plants and animals in stratified formations.

Not only so, but the Bible doesn't imply that Adam had a navel, for the lack of this mark of foetal connection with a mother would hardly have constituted Adam an imperfect being. By the same token, the first trees did not necessarily have growth rings within them, unless it can be shown that these would be essential to the life of a tree. We may be assured that God did *not* create a world filled with unmistakable and essentially unnecessary testimonies to a previous history simply for the purpose of deceiving men! This is why I prefer to use the expression

---

[15]*Omphalos: An Attempt to Untie the Geological Knot* (London: John van Voorst, 1857).

[16]Ibid., p. 347.

[17]*History: Its Purpose and Method* (New York: Harper Torchbooks, 1965), p. 126.

"superficial appearance of age" to describe the original creation. In the last analysis, however, Scripture alone must serve as our guide for determining what God actually did create, in the Biblical sense of that term.

In Genesis 1:11, God commanded the earth to "bring forth . . . the fruit tree yielding fruit after his kind, whose seed is in itself." How are we to understand this? For a number of years I could agree with those who insist that here, at least, we have Biblical evidence for process in creation.[18] However, further study of the Biblical text has led me to abandon this position. The proper context for understanding the events of creation week is not our present world of noncreative process (first law of thermodynamics), but rather the person and work of the Lord Jesus Christ as unveiled in the New Testament. If nearly every visible miracle performed by our Lord on earth involved the creation of built-in history, should we expect anything less during that unique period when He brought the world into existence? When He commanded the earth to bring forth fruit trees, did He have to create seeds first and then wait a number of years for them to grow to maturity? It would be much more in harmony with His later works in the Holy Land to understand this command as being fulfilled by a sudden appearance of full-grown fruit trees bearing fruit. Doubtless it will be objected that this is contrary to God's way of bringing fruit trees into existence today. Quite true! But if this line of argument were pursued consistently, then God could not have created the first seeds either, for if natural observation be our guide, the seeds of fruit trees can only come from fruit trees.

It is really quite impossible to escape the conclusion that if God created living things *after their kind,* as the first chapter of Genesis states ten different times, He must have created them with a superficial appearance of age. And the Scriptures inform us that God began the cycle

---

[18]cf. Russell Mixter, *Evolution and Christian Thought Today* (Grand Rapids: Eerdmans, 1959), pp. 69, 151.

FRUIT TREES

Fruit trees are not the end products of a billion years of evolutionary development from marine protozoans. Instead, they were created by God two days before any marine life appeared, along with all other kinds of plants. Neither did they grow from seeds, but were created full-grown (without growth rings). God did create seeds, but they were inside of fruits hanging from full-grown trees ("and the fruit tree yielding fruit after his kind, whose seed is in itself" Gen. 1:11). Similarly, the first human beings neither evolved from ape-like ancestors nor did they grow up from fertilized eggs or babies. They were created full-grown (without navels), fully capable of obeying God's command to "be fruitful, and multiply, and fill the earth" (Gen. 1:28). The only concept of origins that truly fits the observable facts of genetics and paleontology is supernatural creationism, whereby vast numbers of distinct and unique kinds of living things suddenly appeared with the capacity of reproducing after their kind. Compromise positions, such as theistic evolution, neither fit the clear statements of Scripture nor the discoveries of empirical science.

of life with adult organisms rather than with embryonic forms. Both Old and New Testaments concur in the supernatural creation of Adam and Eve, as adults. And must not this have been true also of all the kinds of animals? How could such creatures have existed as mere fertilized eggs outside of the mother's womb? And how could infant mammals have survived without a mother's care? God would have had to intervene directly and continually to care for them. Therefore, unless we appeal to an endless supplying of miracles, the direct creation of *adult* organisms remains as the only logical interpretation of the Genesis account of the creation of living things *after their kind*.

Recently, this position has been attacked by Dr. Thomas H. Leith in a paper entitled, "Some Logical Problems With the Thesis of Apparent Age," which he presented at the Nineteenth Annual Convention of the American Scientific Affiliation in August, 1964.[19] In the first place, Dr. Leith claims that such a doctrine lacks empirical evidence and undermines all true science. But if this is true, then all miracles in the Bible can be denied, for on the same basis it could be claimed that the virgin birth of Christ lacks empirical evidence and undermines the sciences of genetics and biology. He dismisses the raising of Lazarus as an analogy for creation with apparent history, for in this case, he claims, human observers were present to see the miracle, whereas the supposed discontinuities of Genesis (such as Creation and the Flood) were not observed! Presumably for Dr. Leith the Book of Genesis is not as historically dependable as the Gospel of John, or at least the creative acts recorded in the first two chapters of Genesis do not fit proper standards for empirical verification because human observers were not present to study them. In other words, he seems to be implying that God is not a trustworthy witness of what happened at the time of creation.

---

[19]*Journal of the American Scientific Affiliation*, December 1965, pp. 118 ff.

Dr. Leith's second main objection to the doctrine of apparent age is that it makes God a deceiver of men. "One wonders," he asks, "why deity should be so malevolent (like a Cartesian demon) as to fool us on such interesting matters as much of the history of past events and the possible ages of many things, especially when it is the sort of delusion from which we poor mortals cannot escape!"[20] To this rather common objection, we need only reply that God has not deceived us in such matters if He has given us a Book to tell us what He has done. We have no one to blame but ourselves if we reject the written record of His creative and miraculous works in history. Twenty years ago, Edward J. Carnell suggested two principles to guide us in this area: (1) "since we have God's promise to sustain a regular universe, a Christian could defend the principle of uniformity until he either falls into absurdity or departs from Scripture; (2) we must cheerfully admit God's moral right to create things which only appear, but are not actually, old. The limits of how God has employed this privilege must be measured — in the last analysis — not from science, but from Scripture." We concur with his final conclusion: "These two principles may be hard to apply. True. But there is one thing which is much harder, and that is to rescue Christianity from the jaws of science once the principle of uniformity destroys God's right to perform miracles."[21]

If Scripture be our standard in all truth, then creation with appearance of age is not deceptive, but glorious. Did Jesus deceive the ruler of the feast when He changed water to wine? The Word of God provides the answer for us: "This beginning of miracles did Jesus in Cana of Galilee, and *manifested forth his glory*" (John 2:11). The glory of Christ was revealed in this miracle because it involved

[20]Ibid., p. 122.

[21]"Beware of the New Deism," *His Magazine,* December 1951; see also the answer to Dr. Leith by Lloyd G. Multhauf, Department of Physics, Pennsylvania State University, *Journal of the American Scientific Affiliation,* June 1966, p. 63.

2

the creation
of the universe

W e have seen that the Word of God teaches the supernatural and instantaneous creation of all things. With regard to physical entities in particular, we may add the
concept that no preexistent materials were used. In the
strictest sense, this is the meaning of Hebrews 11:3 —
"By faith we understand that the worlds [*aiōnas*, the
time-space universe] were framed by the Word of God,
so that what is seen hath not been made out of things
which appear" (cf. Rom. 4:17). This certainly cannot
mean that the physical substances that compose our visible universe consist of "invisible" atomic particles! Spiritual faith is certainly not required to accept the atomic
theory of matter in its current form! The point of this
key verse on creationism is that visible material substances
did not exist in any form whatsoever, other than in the
mind of an omniscient God, until He spoke the creative
Word.

The informed and spiritually-minded Christian frankly
acknowledges, in conformity with the clear statement of
Hebrews 11:3, that his understanding of the order of
events and the methods employed by the Creator in bringing the world into existence is basically a *faith-commitment* to God's special revelation. It is "by faith," not by
empirical observation, that he "understands" the *ex nihilo*
approach to ultimate origins. And his confidence in the
absolute authority and dependability of God's written revelation in the Bible is based, in turn, upon a profound
assurance that his Lord, Jesus Christ, who put His divine
imprimatur upon the Scriptures, was neither deceived nor a
deceiver, but spoke final truth (cf. John 14:6; Matt. 5:18;
John 5:46).

At the same time, and in complete honesty, the non-
Christian scientist must acknowledge that *he also* comes to
the factual, observable phenomena with a set of basic assumptions and presuppositions that reflect a profound
"faith-commitment." No scientist in the world today was

present when the earth came into existence, nor do any of us have the privilege of watching worlds being created today! Therefore, the testimony of an honest evolutionist could be expressed in terms of the same Hebrews 11:3 outline, as follows: "By faith, we evolutionists understand that the worlds were *not* framed by the word of any god, so that what is seen has indeed been made out of previously existing and less complex visible things, by purely natural processes, through billions of years."

Thus, it is not a matter of the *facts* of science versus the *faith* of Christians! The fundamental issue, in the matter of ultimate origins, is whether we will put our trust in the written Word of the personal and living God who *was* there when it all happened, or else put our trust in the ability of the human intellect, unaided by divine revelation, to extrapolate presently observed processes of nature into the eternal past (and future). *Which faith* is the most reasonable, fruitful, and satisfying? The author, who was an evolutionist while taking courses in geology and paleontology at Princeton University in 1942-43, finds the Biblical concept of origins to be by far the most satisfying, in every respect.

Christians who truly desire to honor God in their thinking must not come to the first chapter of Genesis with preconceived ideas of what could or could not have happened (in terms of current and changing concepts of uniformitarian scientism). We are not God's counselors; He is ours! "For who hath known the mind of the Lord? or who hath been his counsellor?" (Rom. 11:34) ". . . For my thoughts are not your thoughts, neither are my ways your ways, saith the Lord. For as the heavens are higher than the earth, so are my ways higher than your ways, and my thoughts than your thoughts" (Isa. 55:8-9).

The Creation of the Heavens

For convenience of human thought and expression, the Bible refers to three different heavens. The *third* heaven is that glorious place surrounding the immediate presence of God, to which Paul was carried in a transcendent vision early in his Christian experience (II Cor. 12:1-4). The *second* heaven seems to be equivalent to what we call "outer space"; while the *first* heaven consists of the atmospheric blanket surrounding the earth, in which clouds move and birds fly.

In the first chapter of Genesis, a distinction may be seen between the first heaven, above which the waters were lifted (vss. 8, 20) and the second heaven in which the luminaries were placed (vss. 14-17). There is certainly nothing crude or "prescientific," in the bad sense of that expression, about the cosmology of Genesis, as many able expositors have successfully and repeatedly demonstrated.[1]

What were the "heavens" like at the moment they came from the Creator's hand "in the beginning"? The *third* heaven was populated with hundreds of millions of angelic beings (Dan. 7:10), each one a "son of God" in the sense of a direct creation by God (cf. Job 1:6) and therefore perfect in all their ways (Ezek. 28:15). They must have been created at the very beginning of the first day of creation, for Job 38:6, 7 tells of their singing and of their shout of joy at the creation of the earth.

That they did not exist *before* the first day is indicated by Colossians 1:16 (which tells us that Christ created all *invisible* as well as visible thrones, dominions, principalities and powers *in the heavens* as well as upon the earth) in the light of Exodus 20:11 (*"in six days* Jehovah made heaven and earth, the sea, and *all that in them is"*). (Compare also Ps. 33:6 and Ezek. 28:13, 15.)

The *second* heaven, the realm of "outer space," was presumably empty and dark, for the sun, moon, and stars were not created until the fourth day, and the special light source which divided the light from the darkness had not yet been spoken into existence.

The *first* heaven, or atmospheric blanket, had neither va-

---

[1]cf. R. Laird Harris, "The Bible and Cosmology," *Bulletin of the Evangelical Theological Society,* March 1962, pp. 11-17.

THE OCEANS

The ocean basins of our present world, since the Flood, are much deeper than those before the Flood, because they now serve as reservoirs for "the waters which were above the firmament" as well as "the waters which were under the firmament" (Gen. 1:7). When "the windows of heaven were opened" by God at the beginning of the Flood year, the vast vapor canopy condensed and collapsed in the form of torrential rains within six weeks (Gen. 7:11-12). Then the great mountain ranges rose and the enormous oceanic "valleys sank down" (Ps. 104:8, ASV) so that "the waters returned from off the earth continually" when "the fountains of the deep . . . were stopped" (Gen. 8:2-3). This did not require millions of years, for the waters "fled" and "hasted away . . . unto the place which thou hast founded for them" (Ps. 104:7-8). The sign of the rainbow assures us that the oceans will never again cover the earth (Gen. 9:8-17; Ps. 104:9; Isa. 54:9). Therefore, the oceans have at last reached their final resting place. When the present earth is replaced by a new earth, there will be "no more sea" (Rev. 21:1).

por canopy nor clouds, for the waters were not yet lifted above the expanse ("firmament") in the form of a vast, invisible thermal vapor blanket, as must have existed until the Flood, and there were no clouds or rain as in our present post-Flood world. Neither Genesis nor geology gives any support to the idea that earth's primitive atmosphere consisted of ammonia, methane, hydrogen, and water, as the evolutionary theory of spontaneous generation of life requires (see page 47).

Some Bible students believe that the heavenly bodies were created in the beginning, but could not be seen from the earth because of a cloud blanket so dense that darkness covered the face of the deep. However, the waters were not lifted up until the second day, and the light that was created on the first day was clearly visible from the earth. Also, if God's work on the fourth day involved merely the unveiling of previously created heavenly bodies, this idea could have been more clearly expressed by the use of the verb *appeared* as in verse 9 — "and let the dry land *appear*." Instead of this, we are told that God "made" two great lights on the fourth day, and that He "made" the stars also.

The Creation of the Earth

The earth, like the heavens, was created without the use of preexistent materials (Heb. 11:3), which clearly implies that it was created instantaneously as a dynamic, highly complex entity. It was spinning on its axis, for in reference to the light source created on the first day, it passed through a night-day cycle. It had a cool crust, for it was covered with water.

The crust, however, had no significant features, such as continents, mountains, and ocean basins, for these were formed on the third day. Nor did it have sedimentary and fossil strata, for these were basically the effects of the great Deluge. But it did contain all of the basic elements and the foundational rocks of our present earth.

As a planet, it was perfect in every way, but at this stage of creation week it was not yet an appropriate home for man. It was "without form and void" (*tohu wabohu*). (See chapter 5 for a discussion of the Gap Theory of Genesis 1:2.)

God, of course, could have filled the earth with living creatures on the first day; but Exodus 20:11 suggests that He did it in six days in order to provide a glorious pattern for man's work week. Therefore, we must not judge the quality of God's creative work by the appearance of the earth at the end of the first day. It was merely the first of six twenty-four-hour stages of creation.

Did the Earth Come from a Proto-sun?

If Genesis teaches that the earth was created *before* the sun, moon, and stars, then Christians who believe the Book of Genesis are obviously in serious conflict with evolutionary theory at this point. For this reason, many Christians feel that Genesis must be interpreted in such a way as to avoid this conflict. After all, is it not perfectly clear from astronomical studies that the earth and the other planets came from the sun or from a proto-sun? It shall be our purpose in the following paragraphs to show that this is not true.

By 1940, all the various encounter or planetesimal theories, which postulated the near approach of another star to our sun, resulting in the drawing off of embryonic planets, had been discarded as hopelessly inadequate explanations of the origin of the solar system.[2] In more recent years, Von Weizsacker, Whipple, Spitzer, Urey, Gamow, Hoyle, Kuiper, and others have attempted to avoid the difficulties of the planetesimal theories by returning to a form of nebular hypothesis, whereby the sun and its planets supposedly condensed out of swirling eddies of cold, dark, interstellar clouds of gas and dust. How well this

---

[2]cf. W. M. Smart, *The Origin of the Earth,* rev. ed. (Baltimore: Penguin Books, Inc., 1959), pp. 179-207.

THE GREAT GALAXY IN ANDROMEDA

"He made the stars also" (Gen. 1:16). This gigantic spiral galaxy composed of scores of billions of individual stars is the only one outside of our own Milky Way that is visible to the unaided eye in the Northern Hemisphere. It is two million light years (ten quintillion miles!) away from the earth. Nevertheless, its light rays were created by God already reaching the earth (Gen. 1:15) so that its God-intended function of serving as one of the heavenly "signs" of God's glory and handiwork (Gen. 1:14, Ps. 19:1) and as one of the "clearly seen" testimonies to His eternal power and divinity (Rom. 1:20) could be effectively accomplished. God did not have to create this galaxy two million years beforehand in order for its light to have sufficient time to reach the eye of man. Professor Harold S. Slusher of the Department of Physics and Astronomy, the University of Texas at El Paso, has presented impressive evidences for a comparatively recent origin of the universe in the *1971 Annual of the Creation Research Society* (c/o Wilbert Rusch, 2717 Cranbrook Road, Ann Arbor, Michigan 48104).

currently popular theory succeeds in explaining the solar system in terms of physical, chemical, and mathematical principles alone may be judged by the Christian for himself after considering some of the basic problems which remain to be solved by evolutionary cosmogonists:

First, before any condensation of gas and dust could occur, the nebula would have diffused into outer space. Dr. Gerard P. Kuiper, a leading proponent of the evolutionary concept, admits that before gravitational attraction would become significant, the particles would have to be as big as the moon.[3]

Second, the theory demands a complex system of roller-bearing eddies of gas and dust, but this is impossible because such vortices must remain perfectly intact during essentially the entire period of planetary accretion. But Dr. Kuiper confesses that "it is difficult to conceive that the beautiful system of vortices would actually have been in existence long enough — even for 10 or 100 years — to get the condensation of the building material for the planets under way." Yet the theory demands many *millions* of years.

Third, what stopped the process from continuing so that the entire mass of material did not form one large body? The sun makes up 99 and 6/7 percent of the mass of the solar system, so what would have kept the remaining 1/7 of 1 percent from falling into the main body?

Fourth, other suns do not seem to be condensing or developing planetary systems. There is much interstellar material in the vicinity of our sun, but it is not condensing. Greenstein of the Mount Wilson Observatory is of the opinion that the known stars rotate so fast that one must conclude that they could never have been formed by a condensation process. David Layzer, professor of astronomy at Harvard University, says that there is no known

---

[3]cf. John C. Whitcomb, Jr., *The Origin of the Solar System* (Nutley, N.J.: Presbyterian and Reformed Pub. Co., 1964) for full documentation.

solution to the problem of the small angular momentum (the property that keeps the sun rotating and keeps the planets revolving around it) of the sun. If it had been part of a gaseous protogalaxy, its angular momentum would have to have been a billion times as much as it now possesses. How it could have lost all but 1/10,000,-000 of 1 percent of its original angular momentum has never been explained.[4]

Fifth, the planets contain less than 1 percent of the mass of the solar system but a staggering 98 percent of its angular momentum. David Bergamini, in the *Life Nature Library* volume on *The Universe,* observes: "A theory of evolution that fails to account for this peculiar fact is ruled out before it starts" (p. 93).

Sixth, evolutionary theory cannot explain why seven of the nine planets have direct rotation in reference to their revolution around the sun, but Venus rotates slowly backwards, and Uranus rotates at a 98-degree angle from its orbital plane, even though its orbit inclines less than that of any other planet. Professor Layzer states: "It is an open question whether this state of affairs is consistent" with current theories of the origin of the solar system.

Seventh, evolution has no real answer to the problem of retrograde satellites. Of the thirty-two moons in our solar system, eleven orbit in directions opposite that of the rotational direction of their mother planets. Of special interest is Triton, the inner of Neptune's two satellites, which has nearly twice the mass of our moon (its diameter being 3,000 miles) and which revolves *backwards* every six days in a nearly circular orbit only 220,000 miles from Neptune (closer than our moon to the earth)!

Isaac Asimov, as well as most evolutionary cosmogonists, believes that Triton "was thrown away from that planet by some cosmic collision or other accident," and that later on Neptune recaptured its lost moon into a retrograde or-

[4]"Cosmogony," *McGraw-Hill Encyclopedia of Science and Technology,* 15 vol. (New York: McGraw-Hill, 1960), III, 506.

THE MOON

"The lesser light to rule the night" (Gen. 1:16) remains a faithful witness in the sky to the creative power of God (Ps. 8:3), and at the same time a hopeless enigma to evolutionists, even after several fantastically expensive lunar probes and a close scrutiny of moon rocks. If the moon has been moving through space for millions of years it should have accumulated an enormous depth of meteoritic dust. But the astronauts were amazed to discover less than an inch of dust on the moon's surface. No current theory of its origin commands wide respect among astronomers. It could not have condensed from interstellar dust, for such particles would lack the necessary gravitational attraction. It could not have come out of the earth, or have been captured by the earth, for such concepts are hopelessly contradicted by basic laws of celestial mechanics. The only satisfactory explanation of the moon's existence is that God created it.

bit by "a similar accident."[5] But how many such "accidents" may one be permitted to invoke to prop up a theory already tottering under the weight of its own unproved assumptions? Asimov further states that retrograde satellites are "minor exceptions" to the general rule of satellite orbits. However, eleven out of thirty-two moons having retrograde orbits can hardly be brushed aside as "minor exceptions."

Eighth, what can evolution really offer as an explanation of the angular momentum in these satellite systems? We will permit Professor Layzer of Harvard to state the problem: "Except in the Earth-Moon system (which is exceptional in other respects as well), the primary carries the bulk of the angular momentum, instead of the satellites. . . . This circumstance aggravates the theoretical difficulty presented by the slow rotation of the Sun, for if the Sun has somehow managed to get rid of the angular momentum it would be expected to have, according to the nebular hypothesis, why have the planets not done likewise?"

Ninth, in spite of some ingenious and very complicated theories, it has never satisfactorily been shown why the earth is composed of such heavy elements. In the words of Professor Fred Hoyle of Cambridge University: "Apart from hydrogen and helium, all other elements are extremely rare, all over the universe. In the sun they amount to only about 1% of the total mass. . . . The contrast [with the heavy elements which predominate in the earth] brings out two important points. First, we see that material torn from the sun would not be at all suitable for the formation of the planets as we know them. Its composition would be hopelessly wrong. And our second point in this contrast is that it is the sun that is normal and the earth that is the freak. The interstellar gas and most of the stars are composed of material like the sun, not like

---

[5]*The Intelligent Man's Guide to Science,* 2 vol. (New York: Basic Books, Inc., 1960) I:78.

the earth. You must understand that, cosmically speaking, the room you are now sitting in is made of the wrong stuff. You yourself are a rarity. You are a cosmic collector's piece."[6]

In the light of all these facts of astronomy, evangelical scientists have no right to lend their support to evolutionary cosmogonies. An all-too-typical example of such support appeared in an article in the evangelical *Journal of the American Scientific Affiliation,* which praised Kuiper's gas-dust nebular theory as "truly simple." The author concluded his article with these words: "It is also most gratifying that this process of planetary formation is but a special case of the universal process of binary-star formation, which seems to be one of God's universal Laws. . . . Truly God is in His Universe, and all will be right with the world."[7]

In contrast to this attitude, which presumably is quite widespread among evangelical scientists, the most rational way to explain the origin of our vastly complex solar system is in terms of a direct creation by God. And if this be a reasonable position within the revealed frame of reference of Biblical theism and in view of the conspicuous failures of evolutionary alternatives, may not the supernatural origin of the astronomic system we know the best serve as a model for the supernatural origin of the stellar systems that lie beyond our own?

In other words, if God created *ex nihilo* the two great lights that rule the day and night, He could also have created *ex nihilo* "the stars also." In the words of Dr. Paul A. Zimmerman: "The Biblical account of creation by Almighty God has not been disproved by science. It remains today, even from the viewpoint of reason, I believe, the

---

[6]*Harper's Magazine* (April, 1951), p. 64. Quoted by Paul Zimmerman in *Concordia Theological Monthly* (July, 1953), p. 506.

[7]Jack T. Kent, "The Origin of the Solar System, Galaxy, and the Universe," *Journal of the American Scientific Affiliation,* December 1965, p. 117.

THE SUN

"The greater light to rule the day" (Gen. 1:16) first functioned on the fourth day of a literal creation week, for the verb *made* is used synonymously with *created* throughout Genesis 1. From very ancient times men have been tempted to worship this brilliant creature (Job 31:26; Deut. 4:19), but the fact that God created it *after* the earth and even after plant life demonstrates once for all that the sun is neither indispensable nor ultimate. Furthermore, the sun's enormous and continual loss of mass through nuclear fusion (four million tons a second!) points unmistakably to an original creation when high-level energy and order (low-entropy state) was built into it by God. Thus, the sun provides a magnificent illustration of the second law of thermodynamics and the bankruptcy of cosmic evolutionism. In the new heavens which God will create some day, there will be no further need of the sun (Rev. 21:23; 22:5).

most logical, believable account of the beginning of the earth and the rest of the universe."[8]

The Purpose of the Stellar Creation

Why did God create the sun, moon, and stars on the fourth day rather than the first day? One possible explanation is that in this way God has emphasized the supreme importance of the earth among all astronomical bodies in the universe. In spite of its comparative smallness of size, even among the nine planets, to say nothing of the stars themselves, it is nonetheless absolutely unique in God's eternal purposes.

It was on this planet that God placed man, created in His image, to exercise dominion and to worship Him. It was to this planet that God came in the person of His Son nineteen hundred years ago to become a permanent member of the human race and to die for human sins upon a rugged cross. And it will be to this same planet that this great God and Saviour will return again to establish His kingdom. Because of its positional superiority in the spiritual order of things, therefore, the earth was formed first, and then the stellar systems; just as Adam was first formed, then Eve (I Tim. 2:13).

Another possible reason for this order of events is that God, by this means, made it clear that the earth and life upon it do not owe their existence to the greater light that rules the day, but rather to God Himself. In other words, God was perfectly able to create and take care of the earth and even living things upon it without the help of the sun. Apart from the Scriptures, of course, this would hardly be an obvious fact to mankind.

In ancient times (and even in some parts of the world today) great nations actually worshiped the sun as a god. In Egypt he was called *Re,* and in Babylon he was known as *Shamash.* After all, such worship seemed quite reason-

---

[8]"Some Observations on Current Cosmological Theories," *Concordia Theological Monthly,* July 1953, p. 513.

able in view of the fact that the sun provided light, warmth, and, apparently, life itself.

Even the Jews were greatly tempted to enter into such worship, as may be judged by such passages as Deuteronomy 4:19 and 17:3. Job himself confessed: "If I beheld the sun when it shined, or the moon walking in brightness; and my heart hath been secretly enticed, or my mouth hath kissed my hand: this also were an iniquity to be punished by the judge: for I should have denied the God that is above" (Job 31:26-28).

Perhaps it is not inappropriate to suggest that the evolutionary theory provides a modern and subtle counterpart to the ancient sun-worship cult, for if we must trace our origin to the sun or to a proto-sun, and if we live, move, and have our being exclusively through its boundless blessings and provisions, *then it is our God!*

The creation account in Genesis completely undermines all such blasphemies by putting the sun in a secondary position in reference to the earth. It is not only a mere creature of God, but also a servant to man, the crown of God's creation.

But if the sun, moon, and stars are not ultimately essential to the earth's existence, then why did God create them? Three basic reasons are listed in Genesis 1:14. They are for lights, for seasons (a calendar), and for signs.

As *lights,* they replaced the special and temporary light of the early days.

As a *calendar,* dividing seasons, days, and years, they enable men to plan their work accurately into the distant future, thus reflecting the purposive mind of God.

As *signs,* they teach and ever remind men of vastly important spiritual truths concerning the Creator.

David learned from the heavens the transcendence of God and his own comparative nothingness: "When I consider thy heavens, the work of thy fingers, the moon and the stars which thou hast ordained, what is man that thou art mindful of him?" (Ps. 8:3). The Apostle Paul insisted that men are utterly without excuse for their idolatries, for "the things that are made" give clear testimony to the "everlasting power and divinity" of the Creator (Rom. 1:20).

Apparently, the sun, moon, and stars more effectively accomplish these purposes than one great light source could have. There need be no other reason for their existence than this threefold ministry to man.

But would not this have been an unnecessary waste of God's creative energies? Isaiah gives the effective answer: "Hast thou not known? hast thou not heard? The everlasting God, Jehovah, the Creator of the ends of the earth, fainteth not, neither is weary; there is no searching of his understanding" (Isa. 40:28).

The heavens are the work of God's "fingers" (Ps. 8:3), and when they have fulfilled their God-intended purpose, they will flee away from His face and no place will be found for them (Rev. 20:11). The eternal city will have "no need of the sun, neither of the moon, to shine in it," for the glory of God will lighten it, and the Lord Jesus Christ will be the lamp thereof (Rev. 21:23; cf. 22:5).

Christ and His Word, therefore, must be our final guide as we seek to understand the origin, meaning, and destiny of the heavens and the earth.

3

the creation
of plants and animals

Genesis and the Geologic Timetable

The order of events in the appearance of living things as recorded in the Book of Genesis differs profoundly from that which is generally taught today. Although some writers have sought to draw parallels between the days of Genesis and the various periods of the geologic timetable, it has become increasingly evident that the effort has been unsuccessful. A glance at the Genesis record will show why.

In the first place, Genesis puts the creation of all basic types of land plants (including *fruit trees*) in the *third* day, two days before the creation of marine creatures, whereas evolutionary geologists insist that marine creatures came into existence hundreds of millions of years before fruit trees. Secondly, Genesis tells us that God made the sun, moon, and stars (*made* being clearly synonymous with *created* in this chapter) on the *fourth* day, after the creation of plants, whereas evolutionists assume that the sun existed before the earth itself was formed. Thirdly, Genesis states that the birds were created on the *fifth* day with the fishes, but the geologic timetable has birds following reptiles (which were not created until the sixth day). And finally, Genesis puts the creation of insects ("creeping things") in the *sixth* day, three days after flowering plants were created; but this would be impossible if the days were ages, for pollination requires insects.

Because of such discrepancies, some advocates of this view admit that the "days" may have overlapped each other, and still others have suggested that the order of days in Genesis is topical rather than chronological, serving as a mere literary framework without intending to convey any historical information to the reader. Such revisions and modifications in the once-popular concordist concept simply demonstrate the artificiality of the scheme and its failure in identifying the "days" of Genesis with the periods of uniformitarian geology. Bernard Ramm is probably representative of a number of scholars who have given

the creation of plants and animals • 63

up entirely a literal interpretation of the early chapters of Genesis because of the collapse of concordism, and who now feel that "we must learn to radically rethink creation" in the categories of neoorthodoxy as expressed in the writings of Herrmann, Giersch, and Barth. Dr. Ramm thinks that "a truly Biblical and truly theological notion of creation is going to come from these circles, and not from the surreptitious notion in American orthodox and fundamentalist circles that Genesis 1 is only revelation or inspired if it in some way anticipates modern science." [1]

In refutation of the framework hypothesis of Genesis 1, it may be stated, in the first place, that it finds no place in true Biblical hermeneutics. Dr. Edward J. Young, in his important work entitled, *Studies in Genesis One,*[2] has shown that the early chapters of Genesis bear none of the marks of poetry or saga or myth, but must be interpreted as literally as any other "straightforward, trustworthy history" recorded in Scripture.[3] Furthermore, he demonstrates that the Biblical text calls for a chronological succession of distinct time periods.[4] We have elsewhere pointed out why these time periods must have lasted approximately twenty-four hours. Thus, God never intended to parallel the days of creation with the periods of historical geology.

This leads us to our second basic objection to the framework hypothesis. Like the day-age theory which it has increasingly replaced, it cannot take seriously the perfection of God's completed creation as stated in Genesis 1:31 — "God saw *everything* that He had made, and behold, it was *very good.*" How can we believe, in the light of this statement, that many kinds of plants and animals had already become extinct during the billion or more years of "struggle for existence" that supposedly preceded Adam's

---

[1]"Comments on Mr. Verduin's Essay," *Christianity Today,* May 21, 1965, p. 15.

[2]*Studies in Genesis One* (Nutley, N.J.: Presbyterian and Reformed Pub. Co., 1964).

[3]Ibid., p. 105.

[4]Ibid., pp. 77-100.

creation? Was not Adam told to exercise dominion over "every living thing" (Gen. 1:28) in a unique sense that is no longer true today (cf. Heb. 2:8)? Did not Adam find himself in a world of exclusively *herbivorous* animals (Gen. 1:30; cf. Isa. 11:7)? But the framework theory presupposes that many animals in Adam's day were carnivorous and had been so for hundreds of millions of years. How can this be reconciled with the "groaning and travailing in pain" and "the bondage of corruption" which characterizes the effects of the Edenic Curse upon the animal kingdom *following Adam's fall* (Rom. 8:20-22)?

Bernard Ramm, among others, seeks to solve the problem by redefining the word *good* in Genesis 1:31. "The universe must contain all possible ranges of goodness. One of these grades of goodness is that it can fail in goodness . . . If there were nothing corruptible, or if there were no evil men, many good things would be missing in the universe. The lion lives because he can kill the ass and eat it. . . . The entire system of nature involves tigers and lions, storms and high tides, diseases and parasites."[5] In other words, since it is difficult to imagine any other balance of nature than the one which we observe today, we may assume that the world has always been this way. Dr. G. C. Berkouwer's description of the "harmonistic theodicy" of the Stoics and of the German philosopher Leibnitz (1646-1716) accurately fits this world view. Berkouwer observes: "This theodicy rests principally on a relativizing of sin. God's goodness shines only as the grim clouds of sin and evil are dispelled. . . . Recall, in contrast, how the Scriptures speak of sin as having 'entered into the world' (Rom. 5:12), as 'enmity against God' (Rom. 8:7). The basic error of this theodicy is its fundamental assumption that reason can find a proper place for sin in creation . . . . a fundamental failure to appreciate the awful reality of sin, suffering, and death. Oversimplification

---

[5]*The Christian View of Science and Scripture* (Grand Rapids: Eerdmans Pub. Co., 1954), pp. 93-95.

TWISTED ROCK STRATA
GLACIER NATIONAL PARK, MONTANA

"The mountains went up" (Ps. 104:8, ASV). The context of this passage (i.e., the clear reference to the rainbow covenant in the next verse) makes it obvious that the Holy Spirit is here referring to the gigantic continental uplifts that occurred just after the Flood. Orogeny, or mountain-building, is one of the unsolved mysteries of modern uniformitarian geology; but the Bible supplies the missing dynamic in terms of God's omnipotent intervention at the closing phase of the Flood year. Before the huge sedimentary deposits laid down during the Flood had time to consolidate or solidify they were pushed up to great heights. Still somewhat plastic in consistency, they did not split or shatter when uplifted, but rather were bent and twisted like pages in a thick magazine. This illustrates the important fact that some major geologic features simply cannot be explained in terms of gradual processes over long ages. Natural revelation through science desperately needs the guidelines of special revelation through Scripture if genuine answers to nature's mysteries are ever to be found.

typifies it, and the self-evidency of this oversimplification has contributed to modern man's profound distrust of every attempt at a theodicy."[6]

A third major defect in the concordist and framework hypotheses is that they assume without question the validity of the timetable of uniformitarian geology. This scheme of earth history was devised in the early nineteenth century by men who rejected the Biblical testimony to a universal Flood, and who sought to explain the earth's features in terms of the gradual geologic processes that are observable today.[7] It is obvious, however, that the uniformity principle is completely inadequate for interpreting fluviatile plains, enclosed lake basins, raised river terraces, incised meanders, mountain building, vast horizontal superimposed beds of fossil plants and animals, huge lava plateaus, continental ice sheets, frozen mammoths, and the great reversed-order sequences ("overthrusts") of Montana, Wyoming, and Switzerland. The geologic timetable involves circular reasoning, for it assumes the truth of total organic evolution to arrive at the dates assigned to index fossils and the rocks that contain them. It hardly seems necessary, therefore, to mold Genesis into conformity with a scheme that has failed both logically and experimentally.[8]

The Original Abundance of Life

To those who have been taught to believe that life in the oceans began with a single-celled creature, the Gen-

---

[6]*The Providence of God* (Grand Rapids: Eerdmans Pub. Co., 1952), pp. 238 f.

[7]cf. R. T. Clark and J. D. Bales, *Why Scientists Accept Evolution* (Nutley, N.J.: Presbyterian and Reformed Pub. Co., 1966), p. 19.

[8]cf. John C. Whitcomb, Jr. and H. M. Morris, *The Genesis Flood* (Nutley, N.J.: Presbyterian and Reformed Pub. Co., 1961), pp. 116-211; and N. A. Rupke, "Prolegomena to a Study of Cataclysmal Sedimentation," in *Why Not Creation?* ed. Walter Lammerts (Nutley, N.J.: Presbyterian and Reformed Pub. Co., 1970), pp. 141 ff.

esis account presents an astounding picture: "And God said, Let the waters swarm with swarms of living creatures . . . and God created the great sea-monsters, and every living creature that moveth, wherewith the waters swarmed, after their kind" (Gen. 1:20-21).

It may be noted that in the enumeration of sea creatures in Genesis 1:21 "great sea monsters" ("great whales," KJV) are mentioned first. It is just as if God were intentionally contrasting His great powers of creation with the evolutionary hypothesis which He knew would eventually dominate the world of scientific speculation concerning origins. The blue whale is the largest animal that has ever lived, some individuals attaining a length of 110 feet and a weight of 300,000 pounds. For the God of creation, this was no problem at all, for He created the earth out of nothing by a mere word.

The theory of evolution is deeply embarrassed by the existence of aquatic mammals such as whales, for it must assume that these monsters of the deep evolved from four-legged pig-like land mammals which in turn had evolved from reptiles and fishes. This theory is not only completely lacking in genetic and paleontologic evidence but is logically absurd. Not only so, but the failure of evolutionary theory to account for even the first speck of life has become increasingly evident with the passing of years.

Recently a symposium of papers by some of the world's leading experts on the origin of life was published under the title *The Origins of Prebiological Systems*.[9] One of the papers, presented by Peter T. Mora of the Macromolecular Chemistry Section of the National Institute of Health in Bethesda, Maryland, entitled, "The Folly of Probability," caused considerable debate among the scientists present at the meeting, because he showed that probability statistics offer no hope in explaining the origin of a unicellular organism from inorganic chemicals. "I believe we devel-

---

[9]*The Origins of Prebiological Systems,* ed. S. W. Fox (New York: Academic Press, 1965).

WHALES

Whales, along with all marine creatures, appeared on the fifth day of creation, and thus preceded the land mammals from which they supposedly evolved. The God of creation had no problem launching these monsters of the deep without the help of vast periods of time or previously existing similar forms. But evolutionists have enormous problems explaining how such complex and uniquely structured animals could have evolved into their present forms. To list only three examples out of many: (1) "The female whale gives birth to her young under water, and suckles them under water. The baby whale has its windpipe prolonged above the gullet to prevent milk ejected out of its mother's mammary glands from getting into its lungs. Further, the baby whale's snout is cunningly arranged to fit a receptacle on the body of its mother into which she secretes milk. In this manner the baby whale is prevented from imbibing sea-water with its mother's milk." Could such organs have evolved by random mutations and natural selection? (2) The whale's eye "differs from that of land mammals in having the eyeball immovable, eyelids without eyelashes, no tarsus in the eyelid, a downward direction of eye axis, a more spherical lens, and a greatly thickened sclera." (3) The ear of a whale "is clearly constructed on a different plan from that of the mammalian ear for the reception of air-borne sound waves. The cetacean ear operates in water and is able to resist temporary high pressures when the animal is at depth" (Quotes from Frank Cousins, *Evolution Protest Movement,* No. 114, April, 1964). Evolutionists often point to vestigial hind legs near the pelvis. But these are found *only* in the Right Whale, and upon closer inspection turn out to be strengthening bones to the genital wall. The vast differences between whales and land mammals point infallibly to a separate creation by God.

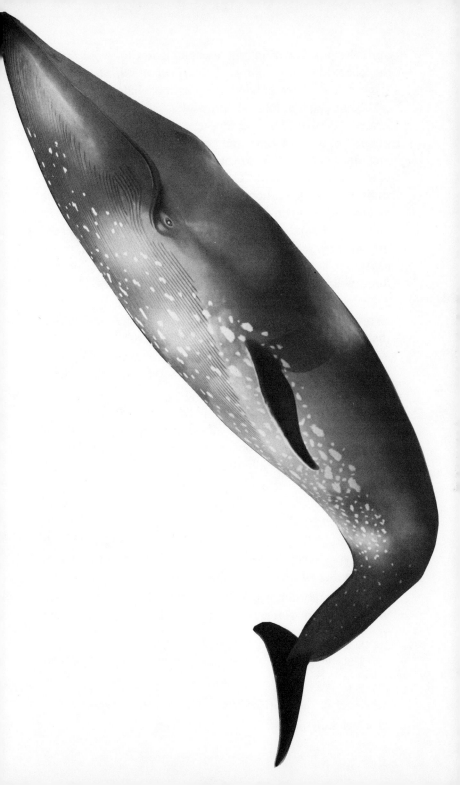

oped the practice of infinite escape clauses to avoid facing the conclusion that *the probability of a self-reproducing state is zero*. This is what we must conclude from classical quantum mechanical principles, as Wigner demonstrated (1961). These escape clauses postulate an almost infinite amount of time and an almost infinite amount of material (monomers), so that even the most unlikely event could have happened. This is to invoke probability and statistical considerations *when such considerations are meaningless*. When for practical purposes the condition of infinite time and matter has to be involved, *the concept of probability is annulled*. By such logic we can prove anything, such as that no matter how complex, everything will repeat itself, exactly and innumerably."[10]

In a review of this symposium entitled, "Did Life Evolve?"[11] R. L. V. Ulbricht strikes hard at the notion that "the origin of life from non-life can be explained by invoking time and chance."[12] He concludes by stating: "The reviewer willingly admits that it is easier to criticize than it is to suggest better alternatives. However, the pace of development in molecular biology is such that in the forseeable future the time will come when the ability of science to solve this problem will become more and more crucial, and failure might mean the beginning of a new revolution in thought."[13] We might add here that the time for this revolution has already come, for a hundred years of rather desperate searching for answers to the origin-of-life problem has ended in complete failure. Multiplying zero creative power by five billion or even an infinite number of years still equals zero results.

In an important work by Malcolm Dixon and Edwin Webb entitled *Enzymes*[14] the authors demonstrate that

---

[10]Ibid., p. 45.

[11]"Did Life Evolve?" *Chemistry and Industry,* January 8, 1966.

[12]Ibid., p. 44.

[13]Ibid., p. 45.

[14]*Enzymes,* 2nd ed. (New York: Academic Press, 1964).

in view of the fact that enzymes can only be formed by other enzymes, there is no known way for life to have started in the first place.[15] After enumerating some of the insurmountable problems in the evolutionary concept, the authors conclude: "A further difficulty is that of holding the components of the system together until a cell membrane is formed, assuming life to have begun in the ocean. Unless the ocean contained throughout a fairly high concentration of the components (thus being itself one gigantic living cell!), the components would rapidly disperse, as happens now when a cell membrane is ruptured. The system would then perish 'by lethal dilution.' But the formation of a cell membrane implies a system which already had a high degree of organization. Thus the whole subject of the origin of enzymes, like that of the origin of life, which is essentially the same thing, bristles with difficulties. We may surely say of the advent of enzymes, as Hopkins said of the advent of life, that it was 'the most improbable and the most significant event in the history of the Universe.' "[16] Thus, Pasteur's demonstration that life can only come from life stands stronger than ever, and the creation account of Genesis is thereby confirmed.

To be sure, vast publicity has accompanied Stanley Miller's experiment in forming amino acids in an apparatus containing methane, ammonia, hydrogen and water and energized by an electric discharge, as evidence that life could have evolved out of inorganic chemicals in the ancient oceans. However, Dr. Duane T. Gish, a former research biochemist at Upjohn Laboratories in Kalamazoo, has pointed out that "the significance of this demonstration is not really very great at all; it might even be termed trivial. Having placed a selected number of gasses in a closed system and supplied a source of energy we would rather be surprised had *not* such a variety of carbon, oxy-

---

[15]Ibid., p. 665.
[16]Ibid., p. 669.

A MONKEY AND A TYPEWRITER

How long would it take lifeless chemicals under ideal conditions to evolve into a living protozoan? Answer: it could *never* happen! Let's simplify the problem. How long would it take a monkey, pounding irrationally at a typewriter, to come up with the words of Genesis 1:1 ("In the beginning God created the heavens and the earth")? In fact, let's allow a million tireless monkeys to pound away at record speed (twelve keys a second) on simplified typewriters with only capital letters. Now, "try to think of a rock so large that if the earth were at its center its surface would touch the nearest star. This star is so far away that light from it takes more than four years to get here, traveling 186,000 miles every second. If a bird came once every million years and removed an amount equivalent to the finest grain of sand, *four such rocks* would be worn away before the champion super simians would be expected to type Genesis 1:1" (Bolton Davidheiser, *Evolution and Christian Faith,* Presbyterian and Reformed Publishing Co., 1969, p. 363; using the calculations of William Feller, *An Introduction to Probability Theory and Its Implications,* Wiley, 1950, I, 266). When the absurdities of evolutionary improbabilities are fed into modern computers, red lights flash and the machinery jams! See Paul S. Moorehead, editor, *Mathematical Challenges to the Neo-Darwinian Interpretation of Evolution* (The Wistar Institute Press, 1967).

gen, and nitrogen-containing compounds been formed."[17] Dr. Gish then refers to a paper by Philip Abelson, Director of the Geophysical Laboratory, Carnegie Institution of Washington, to the effect that such a reducing atmosphere would have been thermodynamically impossible because "an analysis of geologic evidence sharply limits the areas of permissible speculation concerning the nature of the primitive atmosphere and ocean."[18] Dr. Gish concludes: "It is evident, then, that the basis for Miller's experiment did not exist."

Thus, whereas the God of creation was able to create whales and "every living creature that moveth" in a moment of time without exhausting His energies at all, evolutionists cannot imagine how a single-celled self-replicating organism could have been generated spontaneously, even with the kind of reducing atmosphere they have prepared in laboratories and with infinite time at their disposal. Can a greater contrast between two world views be imagined? To state this contrast in different terms, Genesis tells us that *all* the basic kinds of creatures that have ever lived appeared almost simultaneously at the beginning of earth history, and that there have been fewer and fewer kinds ever since, as many have become extinct through the struggle for existence in a world that groans under the bondage of corruption (Gen. 2:1-3; cf. Rom. 8:20-22). On the other hand, the theory of evolution requires one solitary, submicroscopic speck of life at the beginning, with more and more kinds of organisms emerging as the ages come and go. By faith, the evolutionist understands that the organic world was framed by chance in contradiction to present biologic processes. By faith, the Christian understands that the organic world was created by the spoken word of an infinitely powerful, omniscient, per-

[17]"Critique of Biochemical Evolution," in *Why Not Creation?* ed. Walter Lammerts (Nutley, N.J.: Presbyterian and Reformed Pub. Co., 1970), p. 284.

[18]*Abstracts, 133rd National Meeting,* American Chemical Society, April 1958, p. 53.

sonal God as witnessed by the infallible Scriptures and by the obvious discontinuities in the fossil record and in biologic systems today.

The Limits of Variation

It is a foundational principle of the theory of evolution that there can be no fixed limits to the possibility of variation in living things, for the theory assumes that all living things in the world today, both plants and animals, have developed from a single-celled organism. This is the family tree concept of living things, which confronts the student in most textbooks that deal with life sciences, historical sciences, and even world history. There are no institutions of higher learning anywhere in the world today (as far as I am aware) that offer advanced degrees in the natural sciences where the family tree concept of general evolution is rejected. And yet amazingly enough, a century of research on the part of thousands of specialists has failed to produce any clear evidence in contradiction to the Biblical doctrine that living things were created to reproduce after their kind.

Instead of a single family tree of living things, the Bible presents the picture of a great *forest of trees* of living things, each "tree" supernaturally created with the genetic potentialities for variations or branches, but within the strict confines of the created identity of the tree. Thus mankind was created with potentialities for variation into many races, as distinct from each other as the nine-foot Anakim of ancient Palestine and the four-foot Pygmies of central Africa. But there has never been any question that men are men and that the various races belong to the same family tree.

It is apparent that God created certain kinds of animals with an even greater potentiality for variation than is true of mankind. For example, during the past few centuries as many as two hundred breeds of dogs have been developed, as different from each other as the Great Dane and

DACHSHUND AND GREAT DANE

The vast physical and temperamental differences that exist among the nearly two hundred varieties of dogs (all capable of interbreeding) provides for us a perfect illustration of the richness of some God-created gene pools. Spaniels, terriers, beagles, greyhounds, bulldogs, collies, Chihuahuas, chows, and whippets — vastly different in size, shape, color pattern, hair type, and capacities, but all belonging to the same "tree" of dog-kind! Many branches, but *one tree*. God created the DNA code of this "tree" to read D-O-G, and while the world remains, no dog will begin to become a cat, nor will any cat begin to become a dog. If the present world were suddenly overwhelmed by a flood of waters, evolutionary paleontologists of a future age (if evolutionism itself has not become extinct by then!) will doubtless assume that the fossils of dachshunds must be dated a million years earlier than the fossils of Great Danes! In similar fashion, the evolution of the horse and of man have been "reconstructed." Variation within kinds is the exact opposite of evolution, for the boundary lines established by God *can never be crossed* and the new variations that do appear (through gene recombination and sometimes by mutations) represent *an essential weakening* of the individuals in these specialized varieties.

the Dachshund, but they all belong to the same created kind. This is not an evidence for evolution; it is just the opposite, for most of these variations reduce the ability of the animal to survive in nature. It is not primarily by mutations, but rather by *recombination of extant genetic material,* that new races come into existence. As Duyvené de Wit explains, "When a border population is pioneering for a new territory it cannot take along all the genes of its mother-population, but only part of it. Every new race or species which develops from a preceeding one, therefore, owns a *depauperized* gene pool. Hence depletion (decimation) of its gene pool, resulting from genetic drift, is the price which every race and species must pay for the privilege of coming into existence . . . the tragic fate of extremely adapted and specialized species and races, is, therefore, irrevocably: *genetic death.*"[19] Recombination thus subdivides and weakens the genotype and cannot bring about the transformation of one basic genotype into another one.[20]

Although morphology and chromosome count and interfertility are useful methods of identifying distinct kinds of living things, the lines in some cases are not so clearly drawn. Some evangelical scientists, in fact, have made broad concessions to evolutionary theory by suggesting that "God created the orders, and natural selection took it from there," and that "in some cases classes or even phyla could be applied."[21]

At this point, it is important to recognize that the Scriptures do provide some limits as to how inclusive the created kinds really are. In a study of the term *kind* in both

[19]*A New Critique of the Transformist Principle in Evolutionary Biology* (Kampen, Neth.: Kok, 1965), p. 55.

[20]cf. Ernst Mayr, *Animal Species and Evolution* (Cambridge: Harvard University Press, 1963), p. 518; cited by Duyvene De Wit in *A New Critique of the Transformist Principle in Evolutionary Biology* (Kampen, Neth.: Kok, 1965), p. 54.

[21]J. O. Buswell, III, "A Creationist Interpretation of Prehistoric Man," in *Evolution and Christian Thought Today,* ed. Russell Mixter (Grand Rapids: Eerdmans, 1959), p. 183.

Genesis 1 and Leviticus 11, J. Barton Payne concludes that "*min* must refer to subdivisions within the types of life described and not to the general quality of the types themselves."[22] Thus, with regard to Genesis 1, "while *min* does not here require the separate creation by God of each species, it does require at least the separate creation of families within orders." With regard of Leviticus 11, however, Dr. Payne has shown that the kinds of birds are extended at least to genera. "Furthermore, *min* has been shown to be a term for technical enumeration; and it is used in no other, more conversational, way in Scripture. Hebrew lexicons unite in stating that *min* in Scripture has one, and only one meaning, namely 'species.' "[23]

In addition to the limitations on the term *kind* in Leviticus 11, we also have the basic guideline of the size of Noah's ark. The purpose of this structure was to save alive from a universal Flood two of every "kind" of air-breathing creature (Gen. 6:19-20, 8:17). Ernst Mayr estimates that there are about 17,600 species of mammals, birds, reptiles, and amphibians in the world today. Assuming the average size of these animals to be about that of a sheep (there are only a very few really large animals, of course), this would allow room not only for two of each *species* of air-breathing animals in the world today, but also for thousands of species that have become extinct since the Flood. It seems quite obvious, therefore, that Genesis "kinds" cannot be equated with taxonomic "orders" if an ark of such magnitude had to be constructed to provide for two of each "kind."[24]

Some evangelical scientists have insisted that the evolution of the horse family (*Equidae*) provides strong proof that Genesis "kinds" were quite broad. However, G. A.

---

[22]"The Concept of Kinds in Scripture," *Journal of the American Scientific Affiliation*, June 1958, p. 18. See also J. B. Payne, *The Theology of the Older Testament* (Grand Rapids: Zondervan, 1962), p. 137.

[23]Ibid., p. 19.

[24]cf. Whitcomb and Morris, *Genesis Flood,* p. 69.

RAILROAD BOX CARS AND NOAH'S ARK

Noah's ark was the greatest structure ever built to float upon the waters of the seas until the late nineteenth century metal ocean-going vessels were first constructed. It was a barge, not a ship with sloping sides, and therefore had one-third more carrying capacity than a ship of similar dimensions. Assuming the minimum length of the cubit (18 inches), the ark had a capacity of nearly 1,400,000 cubic feet, and was therefore so huge that 522 modern railroad box cars could be fitted inside! And since two each of all air-breathing creatures in the world today could be comfortably carried in only 150 box cars, there was plenty of room in Noah's ark for all the kinds alive today, plus two each of extinct air-breathing types, plus food for them all.

The enormous size of this flat-bottomed, square-sided barge really settles the question of whether the Book of Genesis intends to teach the concept of a universal Flood; for such a structure would not have been needed for saving animals through a localized flood situation. In fact, there would have been no need for an ark at all, for Noah's family (to say nothing of the animals) could easily have been directed by God to migrate to some region unaffected by a local flood. Since God does not give men commands that are foolish or unnecessary, we may be sure that the ark was essential for the survival of air-breathing creatures through this great, year-long catastrophe. See Whitcomb and Morris, *The Genesis Flood,* Presbyterian and Reformed Publishing Company, 1961, pp. 65-70.

HORSES — PRODUCTS OF EVOLUTION?

It has frequently been claimed that fossil horses reveal a clear line of development from the small dog-sized specimens to the large types we see so frequently today. But there is no place in the world where a direct-line fossil sequence from small to large can be found! Therefore, different-sized creatures that had certain horse-like features could have lived contemporaneously in different parts of the world. It cannot be demonstrated that they were all members of the same kind; but even if they were (like the varieties of dogs), this does not prove that they evolved from small to large and from simple to complex. There are many subtle assumptions that underlie the interpretation of fossil finds, not the least of which are *uniformitarianism* (e.g., a gradual deposition of sediments and formation of fossils) and *evolutionism* (an increase of complexity through beneficial mutations). Both assumptions are contradicted by empirical science and an honest exegesis of Scripture. See Frank W. Cousins, "The Unsatisfactory Nature of the Horse Series of Fossils as Evidence for Evolution," *Creation Research Society Quarterly* (September, 1971, pp. 99-108; 2717 Cranbrook Road, Ann Arbor, Michigan 48104).

Kerkut, in discussing the evolution of the horse, says that "the actual story depends to a large extent upon who is telling it and when the story is being told."[25] "At present," states Dr. Kerkut, "it is a matter of faith that the textbook pictures are true, or even that they are the best representations of the truth that are available to us at the present time. One thing concerning the evolution of the horse has become clear . . . instead of a family tree the branches of the tree have increased in size and complexity till the shape is now more like a bush than a tree. In some ways it looks as if the pattern of horse evolution might be even as chaotic as that proposed by Osborn (1937, 1943) for the evolution of the Proboscidea, where, 'in almost no instance is any known form considered to be a descendant from any other known form; every subordinate grouping is assumed to have sprung, quite separately and usually without any known intermediate stage, from hypothetical common ancestors.' "[26] In the light of this, it hardly seems to be a mark of evangelical scholarship to use the supposed evolution of the horse as a basis for determining our definition of Genesis "kinds."

What are some of the limitations to variation in plants and animals that scientists have discovered in the past century? In the first place we have the laws of Mendel which are basic to the science of genetics. It has been said that Darwin would never have won the world to his position if Mendel's discoveries had received the recognition they deserved.[27] These laws explain how variations can normally occur only within fixed limits, in harmony with "after its kind" creation. In the second place, abnormal changes, or "mutations," are practically all harmful or deadly to an organism, as abundantly illustrated in the experiments upon Drosophila fruit flies. George Gaylord Simpson has

[25]*Implications of Evolution* (New York: Pergamon Press, 1960), p. 144.

[26]Ibid., p. 149.

[27]cf. R. E. D. Clark, *Darwin: Before and After* (Chicago: Moody Press, 1967), p. 126.

calculated that "if the mutation rate were .00001 (1 in 100,000 — an average mutation rate) and if the occurrence of each mutation doubled the chance of another mutation occurring in the same cell, the probability that five simultaneous mutations would occur in any one individual would be 1 x 10^{22} (.000000000000000000001). This means that if the population averaged 100,000,000 individuals and if the average generation lasted but one day, such an event as the appearance of five simultaneous mutations in one individual, would be expected once in every 274 billion years."[28] For a discussion of some limitations to variation in plants, see Walter E. Lammerts, "Discoveries Since 1859 Which Invalidate the Evolution Theory."[29]

A third serious limitation on evolutionary variation is the development of complex organs and structures that cannot function until they are complete. Illustrations could be multiplied at great length,[30] but one of the most obvious is the feathered wing of a bird. The majority of evolutionists today, represented by Simpson, Mayr, and Dobzhansky, insist that birds evolved from reptiles through an accumulation of gradual adaptations. But how could this have happened? Are we to suppose that a few reptiles began to develop appendages on the sides of their bodies that grew in size and complexity through the passing millenniums until they finally attained the power of flight? Even granting that a reptile could produce such structures, which is absurd from the standpoint of Mendel's laws, how could such creatures have survived in the struggle for existence? Natural selection would have eliminated them long before they could fly. Furthermore, the

---

[28]*Tempo and Mode in Evolution* (New York: Hafner Pub. Co., 1944), pp. 54 ff.; cited by John W. Klotz, *Genes, Genesis, and Evolution* (St. Louis: Concordia Pub. House, 1955), p. 298.

[29]*Why Not Creation?* ed. Walter E. Lammerts (Nutley, N.J.: Presbyterian and Reformed Pub. Co., 1970), p. 248 ff.

[30]cf. Evan Shute, *Flaws in the Theory of Evolution* (Nutley, N.J.: Presbyterian and Reformed Pub. Co., 1966).

BIRDS

Charles Darwin and his "neo-Darwinist" disciples today have completely failed to explain the origin of birds. Such amazingly adapted creatures could *never* have come into existence by a gradual and chance accumulation of mutations in the bodies of certain reptiles. It is just as ridiculous to imagine that birds were once reptiles as it would be to imagine that airplanes could be produced by attaching wings to the sides of trucks. Flying birds are obviously *designed for flight,* and every minute aspect of their physical form and instinct pattern contributes to this marvellous capacity. Darwin pointed to the different varieties of finches on the Galapagos Islands as "Exhibit A" for evolutionism. But these variations occur within strict limits, and they are all still finches (see Walter E. Lammerts, "The Galapagos Island Finches," in *Why Not Creation?,* Presbyterian and Reformed Publishing Co., 1970, pp. 354-366). At present, there are almost 8,600 distinct species of birds in existence, but there were more in the beginning than there are now. (Note how the "kinds" of birds in Leviticus 11:13-19 closely match our taxonomic "species.") Living kinds can (and many already have) become extinct; but none can ever evolve.

entire structure and instinct pattern of the animal would have to be changed to enable it to take off from the ground. The same problem applies to insects, pterodactyls, and bats. It was once thought that the Archaeopteryx was a link between reptiles and birds, because it had some features of both. But this creature was no more a link between reptiles and birds than the duck-billed platypus is a link between mammals and birds. The Archaeopteryx had full wings and perfect feathers, and no evolutionist has succeeded in explaining where wings and feathers came from.

It was because of problems like these, but especially because no links between major types have been found in the fossil record, that leading paleontologists such as Goldschmidt and Schindewolf finally abandoned the micromutational theory of Neo-Darwinists, and turned to macro-saltations or "typostrophes." Thus, in answer to the question of where the first birds came from, Schindewolf would say: "the first bird crept out of a [mutated] reptile's egg."[31] Such a theory, of course, neatly solves the problem of missing links and natural selection; but from the standpoint of genetics it is a monstrosity, comparable perhaps, to Hoyle's steady-state theory in the light of the first law of thermodynamics. If fully developed birds hatched out of the eggs of reptiles, then perhaps marsupials, placental mammals, and human beings did too!

In answer to this, it might be argued that the doctrine of creation is equally absurd as an alternative to micromutationism, for it involves the sudden appearance of fullgrown birds out of inorganic matter. But this is not a valid objection, for creationism has a dynamic at its disposal that neither Goldschmidt nor Schindewolf had any right to appeal to — *the infinite power of the personal God of creation!* And without God, evolutionists, whether

---

[31]"Der erste Vogel kroch aus einem (abgewandelten) Reptilei," *Grundfragen der Palaontolgie,* Stuttgart, 1950, p. 277; cited in R. Hooykaas, *The Principle of Uniformity* (Leiden: E. J. Brill, 1963), p. 128.

"macro" or "micro," have nothing else to fall back on to provide the necessary dynamic for their theories than the power of *magic*.

Christians who accept by faith the historicity and inerrancy of the Book of Genesis, as taught especially by the Lord Jesus Christ and the Apostle Paul (Matt. 5:18; 19:4; John 10:35; II Tim. 3:16), have no reason to fear that scientific discovery will contradict the Scriptures. Fruit trees could have been created before marine creatures, for the geologic timetable is not an infallible guide to earth history; life began in great abundance, including the largest kinds of animals, for spontaneous generation has failed to provide a logical alternative; and both plants and animals reproduce after their kind, as a veritable forest of independent trees, for the single-tree concept has been shattered by a hundred years of vain search for connecting branches and missing links. When all the facts are in, science will be found to harmonize with the Word of God; but until that day, and while problems and shadows still remain, God would have us take His Word for what He claims it to be — man's only infallible guide to all truth.

4

the creation

of mankind

As he tended his father's sheep by night and gazed into the heavens, David was overwhelmed by the magnitude of God's starry universe. Could a God of such power and transcendence have any real interest in these mere specks of cosmic dust called men? Astronomy as such could provide no comfort for David in this desperately crucial problem; and the fantastic advances in astronomical knowledge we have experienced since his day still leave us in utter darkness. Modern astronomers, peering through gigantic telescopes, have yet to discover a single trace of the grace and love of God anywhere in the universe. All true Christians would agree that the answer to *this* question must come from the inscripturated Word of God and from there *alone*. It was to the first chapter of Genesis that David appealed as his source of assurance that God created man a little lower than Elohim (the realm of deity) and crowned him with glory and honor, giving him dominion over all creation (Ps. 8:5-8; cf. Gen. 1:26-28). In spite of the conspicuous failure of *natural revelation* at this point, however, *special revelation* assures us that the human race *is* the object of God's loving concern, and one human being is more important to God than all the stupendous galaxies of the universe.

Looking carefully about him at a world groaning under the bondage of corruption, the brilliant author of the Book of Ecclesiastes saw no *empirical* basis for distinguishing human beings from beasts. "I saw under the sun . . . that which befalleth the sons of men befalleth beasts; even one thing befalleth them: as the one dieth, so dieth the other: yea they have all one breath; and man hath no preeminence above the beasts: for all is vanity. All go unto one place; all are of dust, and all turn to dust again" (Eccl. 3:19-20). Three thousand years later our scientific advances have not helped us at all in solving this problem. No one can prove experimentally that the spirit of a beast vanishes at death but that the spirit of man lives on forever. From the standpoint of chemistry, a good case could be made for the proposition that man is on the same level with animals. Both are made of the same dust. Modern scientists, peering through powerful microscopes fail to see any trace of the image of God in the chemicals of man's body. All true Christians would agree that the final answer to *this* question also must come from the Bible and from there *alone*. Once again, the first chapter of Genesis is seen to be foundational to our faith, when natural revelation fails us.

But some Christians are not willing to carry this principle of the ultimate authority of Scripture to its logical conclusion. They acknowledge that the Bible, rather than astronomy and chemistry, is our source of information concerning the *dignity* of man. But they cannot bring themselves to believe that the Bible rather than physical anthropology is our source of truth concerning the *creation* of man. Here, at least, we are told, natural revelation has equal authority with special revelation in Scripture, and wherever there is conflict the early chapters of Genesis must be molded into the framework of contemporary scientific theory concerning the origin of man. As one writer recently has expressed it, "Both the Bible of nature and the Holy Bible are infallible, each in its own way, because both are written by the almighty hand of God; otherwise, speaking with all reverence, God could not be trusted. Evolution is not just about all hypothesis. We are compelled to believe that at least much of it is true. And we may not be silent about that. . . . It is the result of reading the Bible of nature directly."[1] Another writes: "I view the opening chapters of Genesis as a poetic expression of the God-inspired author of that book. I believe that this part of Scripture should not be regarded as a scientific textbook. . . . Should not a Christian be permitted to use science to delve into the unsolved mysteries of creation?"[2]

---

[1]Peter G. Berkhout, *The Banner,* March 5, 1965, p. 22.

[2]Robert C. Homan, *The Banner,* October 22, 1965, p. 20.

This viewpoint, which may be called the "double-revelation theory," maintains that God has given to man two revelations of truth, each of which is fully authoritative in its own realm: the revelation of God in Scripture and the revelation of God in nature. Although these two revelations differ greatly in their character and scope, they cannot contradict each other, since they are given by the same self-consistent God of truth. The theologian is the God-appointed interpreter of Scripture, and the scientist is the God-appointed interpreter of nature, and each has specialized tools for determining the true meaning of the particular book of revelation which he is called upon to study.

The double-revelation theory further maintains that whenever there is an apparent conflict between the conclusions of the scientist and the conclusions of the theologian, especially with regard to such problems as the origin of the universe, the solar system, the earth, plant and animal life, and man; the effects of the Edenic Curse; and the magnitude and effects of the Noahic Deluge; the theologian must rethink his interpretation of Scripture at these points in such a way as to bring the Bible into harmony with the general consensus of scientific opinion, since the Bible is not a textbook of science, and these problems overlap the territory in which science alone must give us the detailed and authoritative answers.

Advocates of the double-revelation theory hold that this is necessarily the case, for if an historical and grammatical interpretation of the Biblical account of Creation, the Edenic Curse, the Flood, and the Tower of Babel should lead the Bible student to adopt conclusions that are contrary to the prevailing views of trained scientists concerning origins, then he would be guilty of making God a deceiver of mankind in these vitally important matters. But a God of truth cannot lie. Therefore Genesis must be interpreted in such a way as to agree with the generally-accepted views of modern science. After all, we are reminded, Genesis was written only to give us answers to the questions "Who?" and "Why?" but modern science must answer the important questions "When?" and "How?"[3]

Theistic Evolution

Following this general approach to the early chapters of Genesis, a number of Christian men of science (and probably an even larger number of theologians following in their footsteps) have adopted the view that Adam's body was simply that of some animal which had providentially been evolved into a biped through millions of years of gradual changes until God put within it an eternal soul several hundred thousand years ago. Thus, in *Evolution and Christian Thought Today,* Walter Hearn and Richard Hendry conclude a chapter on "The Origin of Life" with these words: "The authors of this chapter consider the expressions of Scripture regarding the creation of life to be sufficiently figurative to imply little or no limitation on possible mechanisms."[4] In a symposium entitled "Origins and Christian Thought Today," held at Wheaton College on February 17, 1961, Dr. Hearn further clarified his position: ". . . surely we know that processes have been involved in bringing *us* into existence. Why shudder, then, at the idea that processes were involved in bringing Adam into existence? Granted that we do not yet know details of the processes, why may we not assume that God *did* use processes?"[5]

Henry W. Seaford, Jr., testifies that "an evolutionary view of man's place in nature assists my understanding of the antithesis between flesh and spirit. When I instruct my children in morality I can explain that the human body is an animal closely related to other Higher Primates . . . ."[6] Dr. Jan Lever of the Free University of Amsterdam

---

[3]John C. Whitcomb, Jr., *The Origin of the Solar System* (Nutley, N.J.: Presbyterian and Reformed Pub. Co., 1964), p. 8.

[4]*Evolution and Christian Thought* Today, ed. Russell L. Mixter (Grand Rapids: Eerdmans, 1959), p. 69.

[5]*Journal of the American Scientific Affiliation,* June, 1961, p. 42.

[6]"Near-Man of South Africa," *Gordon Review,* Winter 1958, pp. 187-189.

agrees that "when we thus place side by side the knowledge which we possess of the higher life of the Primates of the Pleistocene Epoch and the revelation that man has been brought forth within that which has been created, then we may not reject in advance the *possibility* that the genesis of man occurred by way of a being that, at least with respect to the characteristics of its skeleton, was an animal, according to our norms and criteria . . . we may not reject in advance the possibility that there has existed a genetic relation between man and animal."[7]

Under pressure from these and similar statements by Christian men of science, one prominent evangelical theologian has come to this position: "Since orthodoxy has given up the literal-day theory out of respect for geology, it would certainly forfeit no principle if it gave up the immediate-creation theory out of respect for paleontology. The two seem to be quite parallel. . . . If God was pleased to breathe His image into a creature that had previously come from the dust, so be it."[8] Thus, natural revelation, as interpreted by the scientist, cannot long remain on an equal footing with special revelation in Scripture, but finally supersedes it entirely.

Theistic evolution cannot consistently allow for any physical miracle in Adam's "creation." Thus, even after the image of God was put into a male and a female ape, their bodies, being unaffected by this spiritual miracle, would continue to be subject to disease and death just like the bodies of other apes. Therefore sin could not be the cause of physical death even in the human race, and Romans 5:12 would be incorrect when it tells us that "through one man sin entered into the world, and death through sin."

---

[7]*Creation and Evolution* (Grand Rapids: Grand Rapids International Publications, 1958), pp. 197, 221.

[8]Edward John Carnell, *The Case for Orthodox Theology* (Philadelphia: Westminster Press, 1959), p. 95. See also Harold J. Ockenga, *Women Who Made Bible History* (Grand Rapids: Zondervan, 1962), p. 12.

MANKIND

Man is the crown of God's creation. He was made in the image and likeness of his Creator and was given complete dominion over the earth (Gen. 1:26). "The heavens are the heavens of the Lord: but the earth hath he given to the children of men" (Ps. 115:16). Fallen man has lost that original dominion, but still possesses God's image (Gen. 9:6; James 3:9). Redeemed through Christ, God's incarnate son, believing men have already been moved positionally from the realm of "little lower than angels" (Heb. 2:7) to a realm "far above all principality, and power, and might, and dominion, and every name that is named" (Eph. 1:21; 2:6). Glorified men will even judge angels (I Cor. 6:3).

In the light of all this, how utterly blasphemous is the currently popular idea that man is little more than "a naked ape." *The physical differences* between men and apes are enormous, as Dr. John W. Klotz has shown (in Paul Zimmerman, ed., *Darwin, Evolution, and Creation,* St. Louis: Concordia Pub. House, 1959, p. 128). But if the physical differences are great, *the mental-cultural-spiritual differences* are little short of infinite. Of all living beings on this planet, only man is self-conscious as a person; is sufficiently free from the bondage of instinct to exercise real choices and to have significant purposes and goals in life; has complex emotions including sadness and joy; appreciates art and music creatively; can make real tools; can be truly educated rather than merely trained; can use oral and written symbols to communicate abstract concepts to other persons and thus enjoy true fellowship; can accumulate knowledge and attain wisdom beyond previous generations and thus make genuine history; can discern moral right and wrong and suffer agonies of conscience; can recognize the existence and rightful demands of his Creator through worship, sacrifice, and religious service.

Some theistic evolutionists have frankly recognized the theological implications of their surrender to evolutionary anthropology and have been willing to adjust their theology accordingly. Dr. Peter Berkhout, for example, has stated: "We realize full well, that, if what we call theistic evolution were accepted as true, a tremendous change would take place in our thinking; compared with which the change to the Copernican point of view would be a mere bagatelle. For example, if man did descend from some primate physically, can we attribute all imperfection and all of what we call physical evil to man's Fall? Is it not an oversimplification anyway? Many of our books would have to be rewritten. But if necessary for the sake of truth, why not?"[9] Charles Darwin also traveled down this path. "First of all his faith in the Old Testament was shattered. Then he could no longer believe in the miracles of the New. Finally he was left wondering whether Christianity was a Divine revelation at all."[10]

In order to avoid such theological disaster, the Roman Catholic Church, together with many Protestants today, took refuge in a more modified form of theistic evolution. In his Encyclical "Humani Generis" issued in 1950, Pope Pius XII gave official permission to Roman Catholic teachers to discuss the possibility of "the human body coming from pre-existent and living matter" (Article 64). Because of their dichotomous view of man, this was no great surrender for Catholics. However, the Encyclical did try to hold the line on three points: (1) the original righteousness of Adam and Eve; (2) the historicity of the Fall; and (3) the unity of the race in Adam. The inconsistency of this compromise is obvious. In order for God to change a mortal ape into a sinless and therefore immortal man, who had sufficient vigor to live 930 years even after the Fall, a physical as well as a spiritual miracle had to

[9]"Revelation and Evolution," from a Netherlands publication cited by John Vander Ploeg, *The Banner*, October 8, 1965, p. 9.

[10]R. E. D. Clark, *Darwin: Before and After* (Chicago: Moody Press, 1967), p. 83.

occur. But once we grant the necessity of such a physical miracle in Adam's creation in order to preserve some of the essentials of Christianity, why shouldn't we take the text of Scripture as it stands and grant that God created Adam's body directly?[11]

The Direct Creation of Adam's Body

For those who are willing to search the Scriptures and to believe what they say, nothing can be clearer than the fact that God directly created the bodies of Adam and Eve wholly apart from the use of previously existing animals. Let us begin with the New Testament. When the Pharisees confronted the Lord Jesus Christ with the divorce question (Matt. 19:3), He answered them by asserting the permanence of the marriage bond in terms of Genesis 2:24 — "Therefore shall a man cleave unto his wife: and they shall be *one flesh.*" Now it is important to note that our Lord introduced this reference to the first marriage by appealing to the physical basis for it: "Have ye not read, that he who made them from the beginning made them male and female?" (cf. Gen. 1:27). In opposition to the theistic evolution position, therefore, the Lord Jesus Christ confirmed the teaching of Genesis that God not only created man in His image and likeness (spiritually), but also male and female (physically). If man had been an animal physically before he acquired his spiritual nature, he would *already* have been male and female, and the statements of Genesis 1:27 and Matthew 19:4 would be inaccurate and misleading.

The Apostle Paul certainly agreed with this concept of the physical uniqueness of the human race when he wrote: "All flesh is not the same flesh: but there is one flesh of men, and another of beasts . . ." (I Cor. 15:39). The basic thrust of theistic evolution, of course, is that all flesh

---

[11]cf. J. O. Buswell, "A Creationist Interpretation of Prehistoric Man," *Evolution and Christian Thought Today,* Russell Mixter, ed., 1959, p. 186.

on earth is *the same flesh,* the human race being a mere twig on the branch of anthropoid mammals. Paul's statement is in clear contradiction to this theory.

Perhaps the clearest New Testament statement concerning the supernatural origin of mankind is found in I Corinthians 11:8, 12 — "For the man is not *of* the woman; but the woman *of* the man . . . for as the woman is *of* the man, so is the man also *by* the woman." The preposition *of* (*ek*) has reference here to ultimate physical origin, while the preposition *by* (*dia*) refers to the process of birth. Paul is saying that while all men today are born of women, women had their ultimate origin in a man (compare Gen. 3:20 with Acts 17:26 ASV). But this can only be true if theistic evolution is false, for otherwise the first woman would have come physically from a female animal, not from a man.

Turning now to the Old Testament, we come to the crucial text on man's physical creation, Genesis 2:7 — "And Jehovah God formed man of the dust of the ground, and breathed into his nostrils the breath of life; and man became a living soul." To the extent that theistic evolutionists bother with the Biblical text at all, they insist that "the dust of the ground" from which God formed Adam was *living* "dust" and is thus symbolic of the animal kingdom. Furthermore, we are told that Adam's creation simply involved the impartation of a *spiritual* nature to a subhuman creature, for the Bible says that "man became a living *soul.*"

But the science of Biblical hermeneutics does not permit Genesis 2:7 to be handled in this way! One of the basic laws of this time-honored and God-honored science is the *law of context.* According to this law, each passage of the Bible must be understood in the light of the passages that precede and follow it and ultimately in the light of the entire Bible. Otherwise, a passage could be twisted out of context and be made to teach something that it was never intended to teach. Basically, this is how every heresy and cult throughout church history sprang forth.

Now the context of Genesis 2:7 demonstrates, in the first place, that the phrase "man became a living soul" does not allow for a prehuman form of life for Adam's body. The phrase *living soul* (*nephesh hayah*) should actually be translated "living creature," for the same phrase appears in Genesis 1:20, 21, and is applied to sea creatures! In other words, the purpose of Genesis 2:7b is not to tell us that Adam had a unique soul (which we already learn by implication in Genesis 1:26, 27), but that Adam was not *any* kind of a living creature until he *became* one by the creative breath of God. Until that moment, he was inanimate, lifeless matter. The significance of this fact can hardly be overestimated.

This leads us to a second important discovery from a study of the context, namely, that "dust of the ground" cannot be understood symbolically of animals but must be interpreted literally. Note, for example, the terms of God's curse upon Adam in the following chapter: "Cursed is the ground for thy sake . . . thorns also and thistles shall it bring forth to thee . . . in the sweat of thy face shalt thou eat bread, till thou return to the ground; for *out of it wast thou taken*: for dust thou art, and *unto dust shalt thou return*" (Gen. 3:17-19).

Two interesting things are said here about the "ground" and the "dust" from which Adam was taken: (1) it would bring forth thorns and thistles, and (2) Adam would return unto it. Now if "dust of the ground" symbolizes the animal kingdom in Genesis 2:7, what does it mean here? Does this passage mean that animals brought forth thorns and thistles as a result of the curse? And does it mean that Adam had to return to the animal kingdom when he died? Those who believe in reincarnation might favor the idea that "dust" here includes the animal kingdom, but a theistic evolutionist would hardly want to use this as a prooftext of his "living dust" concept!

Thus, the hermeneutical law of context demands that "dust of the ground" in Genesis 2:7 be interpreted literally, and it completely excludes the possibility of an animal ancestry for man. The second chapter of Genesis also makes it perfectly clear that Eve was taken physically, literally, and supernaturally from the side of Adam. If this point be granted, then the whole purpose of trying to interpret Adam's creation in evolutionary terms falls apart. To connect Adam's body with the animal kingdom but to admit that Eve's body was directly created would be absurd, either from the standpoint of evolutionary science or Biblical creationism. We may not know in exact detail how God fashioned the bodies of our first parents, but that He created them miraculously and suddenly is the plain teaching of Scripture.

One can hardly claim that the facts of science contradict this Biblical doctrine. Duyvené de Wit has shown that the process of raciation and speciation is inevitably bound up with genetic depletion as a result of natural selection, and that when this scientifically established fact is applied to the question whether man evolved from a primate stock, "the transformist concept of progressive evolution is pierced in its very vitals."[12] The reason for this, as Duyvené de Wit goes on to explain, is that the whole process of evolution from animal to man "would have run against the gradient of genetic depletion. That is to say, that, from a genetical viewpoint, man must possess an *unaccountably smaller gene-potential than his animal ancestors!* Here, the impressive absurdity becomes clear in which the transformist doctrine entangles itself when, in flat contradiction to the factual scientific evidence, it dogmatically asserts that man has evolved from the animal kingdom!"[13] In the light of this, what must be said of Christians who surrender the direct creation of Adam and Eve out of respect for the prevailing viewpoints of evolutionary scientists?

---

[12]*A New Critique of the Transformist Principle in Evolutionary Biology* (Kampen, Neth.: Kok, 1965), p. 56.

[13]Ibid., p. 57.

If natural revelation is superseded (but not contradicted) by special revelation with regard to man's true dignity and his supernatural creation, does it not at least provide for us the basis for determining his antiquity? James Oliver Buswell III, a Christian anthropologist who accepts the direct creation of Adam as the clear teaching of Scripture, believes, at the same time, that "the creationist may accept the evidence for the age of pre-historic man and his culture. He need have no quarrel with an antiquity of hundreds of thousands of years; there is nothing in the Bible to indicate how long ago man was created."[14]

When Carl F. H. Henry criticized Christian anthropologists for giving way to "the inordinate pressures of contemporary scientific theory about the antiquity of man,"[15] Buswell replied that he and other anthropologists such as Wilson, Stipe, Smalley, Taylor, Ellenberger, Nickerson, and Rayburn, were simply following William Henry Green and B. B. Warfield in their denial that the genealogies of Genesis placed *any* limitations on the antiquity of man. Buswell concluded: "I'm sure that we Christian anthropologists would be willing to study with an open mind any serious, scholarly attempt to invalidate, overthrow, or supersede the classic works in this area upon which our position partially rests."[16]

In response to this challenge, I would like to suggest several Biblical limitations upon the antiquity of the human race. In the first place, to stretch the genealogies of Genesis 5 and 11 to cover a period of over a hundred thousand years is to do violence to the chronological framework of all subsequent Bible history. By means of Biblical analogies, it is indeed possible to find gaps, especially in the genealogy of Genesis 11. But those very analogies serve to

---

[14]*Evolution and Christian Thought Today,* p. 181.

[15]Editorial, *Christianity Today,* January 15, 1965, p. 28.

[16]Letter to the Editor, *Christianity Today,* March 12, 1965, p. 22.

limit our timescale for Genesis 11. The gap between Amram and Moses was three hundred years, not thirty thousand (cf. Exod. 6:20, Num. 3:17-19, 27-28). And the gap between Joram and Uzziah in Matthew 1:8 was fifty years, not five thousand.[17]

In the second place, only three of the ten patriarchs listed in Genesis 11 — Reu, Serug, and Nahor — are available for spanning the vast period of time demanded by these anthropologists, for the patriarchs listed before them preceded the Tower of Babel judgment and the scattering of mankind (cf. Gen. 10:25). And yet the clearest suggestion of a time gap in Genesis 11 occurs *before* this judgment, between Eber and Peleg, because of the sudden drop of average life span.

In the third place, it is impossible to imagine that Reu, Serug, and Nahor, to say nothing of Lamech, Noah, and Shem, were savage, illiterate cave-dwellers of the stone-age period. The fourth chapter of Genesis, with its clear indication of cultural achievement, including the forging of "every cutting instrument of brass and iron" (vs. 22), and Genesis 6, with its account of the great ark-building project, make such a theory completely untenable. Or are we to suppose that in some tiny pocket of civilization, nearly swamped by an ocean of human savagery, an unbroken chain of saintly men (some of whom lived for centuries) perpetuated the Messianic line of Shem and handed down the knowledge of the one true God for hundreds of thousands of years? Even to ask such a question is to answer it.

Finally, we must ask how certain details of the story of the great Flood could have been handed down from one primitive stone-age culture to another, purely by oral tradition, for hundreds of thousands of years, to be finally incorporated into the Gilgamesh Epic of the Babylonians? That such could have happened for several thousand years

---

[17]See J. O. Buswell's response to this argument in *The Journal of the American Scientific Affiliation*, September 1965, p. 75.

is conceivable. That it could have happened over a hundred thousand years is quite inconceivable. The Gilgamesh Epic alone, rightly considered, administers a fatal blow to the concept of a vast antiquity for Adam and Noah.[18]

It is true that Benjamin B. Warfield was one of the greatest orthodox theologians of modern times. But it is also true that he was capable of making mistakes. One such mistake, we believe, was his assertion that "two thousand generations and something like two hundred thousand years may have intervened" between Adam and Noah as far as the Scriptural data in Genesis 5 and 11 are concerned.[19] It should also be pointed out, however, that Warfield went on to say (and this statement is seldom quoted today) that man has probably not existed on earth more than ten to twenty thousand years.[20] It is unfortunate that Warfield's statement with regard to Genesis 5 and 11 is so frequently appealed to as the final word on the subject of pre-Abrahamic chronology.[21]

One of the disturbing trends in the Church today is the widespread refusal of Christian men of science to challenge the uniformitarian assumptions which underlie various schemes for determining the age of fossils. Why must Christians accept the timetable of evolutionary paleontology and anthropology when it involves a denial of

---

[18]John C. Whitcomb, Jr. and Henry M. Morris, *The Genesis Flood* (Nutley, N.J.: Presbyterian and Reformed Pub. Co., 1961), pp. 483-89.

[19]"Antiquity and Unity of the Human Race" in *Biblical and Theological Studies* (Nutley, N.J.: Presbyterian and Reformed Pub. Co., 1952), p. 247.

[20]Ibid., p. 248.

[21]Henry M. Morris has demonstrated that if the uniformity principle be applied to population growth, the results are impossibly absurd on the basis of a million-year old human race. If the average family had only three children and the life-span was one generation, in a million years there would be fifty times more people than could be crammed into the entire known universe! cf. *Biblical Cosmology and Modern Science* (Nutley, N.J.: Craig Press, 1970), p. 75.

the Biblical doctrine of supernatural creation and also the catastrophic effects of a geographically universal Flood in the days of Noah? The universality of the year-long Deluge is one of the clearest doctrines of Scripture, supported by many and varied arguments; and yet we find many evangelical scientists ignoring or denying this doctrine in their surrender to uniformist concepts of earth history. As one has expressed it, "an honest creationist will ask the paleontologist what he knows of the time of origin of animals, and draw his conclusions from the data."[22] When the paleontologist Leakey suggested a date of 1,750,000 years for a human fossil he discovered, Buswell found no particular problem of accommodating Genesis 5 and 11 to this new chronology (again appealing to Warfield), and in "correspondence with other creationist anthropologists in direct solicitation for opinion about *Homo habilis* . . . the responses indicated a general lack of alarm at the increased antiquity."[23] Such men may see no problem in allowing 100,000 years between *each* of the twenty patriarchs of Genesis 5 and 11, but for most Bible-believing Christians this is an utter absurdity. Even as our understanding of the dignity and supernatural creation of man rests upon the clear terms of special revelation, so also our understanding of *the basic outline of man's earliest history* must come from Scripture rather than from science.[24]

The fact that the first eleven chapters of Genesis cannot be harmonized with evolutionary schemes of earth history is evidenced by the fact that liberal and neo-orthodox scholars have long since given up the effort of taking those chapters as serious history.[25] It is the privilege of these

---

[22]*Evolution and Christian Thought Today,* p. 183.

[23]*Journal of the American Scientific Affiliation,* September 1965, p. 77.

[24]For a helpful discussion of human fossils, see Arthur C. Custance, "Fossil Man in the Light of the Record in Genesis," in *Why Not Creation?* ed., Walter Lammerts (Nutley, N.J.: Presbyterian and Reformed Pub. Co., 1970), pp. 194-229.

[25]cf. Ralph H. Elliott, *The Message of Genesis* (Nashville: Broadman Press, 1961).

men to dispense with an historical Adam if they so desire. But they do not at the same time have the privilege of claiming that Jesus Christ spoke the truth. Adam and Jesus Christ stand or fall together, for Jesus said: "If ye believed Moses, ye would believe me. But if ye believe not his writings, how shall ye believe my words?" (John 5:46-47). Our Lord also insisted that "till heaven and earth pass away, one jot or one tittle shall in no wise pass from the law [*and this includes Genesis*] till all things be accomplished" (Matt. 5:18). If Genesis is not historically dependable, then Jesus is not a dependable guide to all truth, and we are without a Saviour.

The Apostle Paul said that "as through one man's dis-obedience the many were made sinners, even so through the obedience of the one shall the many be made righ-teous" (Rom. 5:19); and "as in *Adam* all die, so also in *Christ* shall all be made alive" (I Cor. 15:22). If Adam didn't fall from original righteousness, then there is no sin, and Christ died for nothing. If universal death through Adam is a myth, then so is the doctrine of the resurrec-tion, and the Apostle Paul is a false witness (I Cor. 15:15). The full historicity of the Genesis account of Adam and Eve is absolutely crucial to the entire God-revealed plan of salvation.

Surely the words of rebuke given by our Lord to the two on the road to Emmaus must be applicable to many Christians today: "O fools and slow of heart to believe all that the prophets have spoken" (Luke 24:25). Our basic problem today in the question of origins is not so much that we are ignorant of the theories and speculations of men. Our problem too often is that we neither know the Scriptures nor the power of God, and therefore deeply err in communicating God's message to modern man. May God be pleased to grant to each of us a renewing of our minds through submission to His special revelation of truth in His infallible Word, that we might prove what is that good and acceptable and perfect will of God.

5

**was the earth
once a chaos?**

The Basic Issue

Conservative students of the Bible have long debated the question of whether the original creation of the heavens and the earth is to be understood as an event within the first "day" of creation, or whether a vast period of time could have elapsed between the original creation of Genesis 1:1 and the "waste and void" condition described in Genesis 1:2. Most Christians who favor a time gap between these two verses believe that the original earth was populated with plants and animals (and perhaps even pre-Adamic "men"), and because of the fall of Satan it was destroyed by God through means of a global flood, was plunged into total darkness, and thus *became* "waste and void." The vast ages of the geologic timetable are thought to have occurred during this interval, so that the fossil plants and animals which are found in the crust of the earth today are relics of the originally perfect world which was supposedly destroyed *before* the six literal days of creation (or, rather, re-creation) as recorded in Genesis 1:3-31.

The "gap theory" (or "ruin-reconstruction theory") has been widely accepted among evangelical Christians, especially since the early nineteenth century when Dr. Thomas Chalmers of Scotland popularized this interpretation, presumably with the motive of harmonizing the Genesis account of creation with the vast time periods of earth history demanded by uniformitarian geologists.[1] The theory

---

[1]Although the Gap Theory had been advocated in one form or another spasmodically for centuries (see documentation in Arthur Custance, *Without Form and Void,* Box 291, Brockville, Ontario, Canada, 1970), it was first popularized by Dr. Thomas Chalmers of Edinburgh University in 1814. In this way he attempted to incorporate Georges Cuvier's concepts of geologic catastrophism into a Biblical framework. See *The Works of Thomas Chalmers on Natural Theology* (Glasgow: Wm. Collins and Co., n.d.); Bernard Ramm, *The Christian View of Science and Scripture* (Grand Rapids: Eerdmans, 1954), pp. 195 ff.; Francis Haber, *The Age of the World* (Baltimore: Johns Hopkins Press, 1959), pp. 201 ff.; Erich Sauer, *The King of the Earth* (Grand Rapids: Eerdmans, 1962), pp. 230 ff.

was elaborated in 1876 by George H. Pember (*Earth's Earliest Ages*), and then enormously popularized in the footnotes of the *Scofield Reference Bible* beginning in 1917. Recently, Arthur C. Custance, a Canadian scientist, has published a careful defense of the Gap Theory entitled, *Without Form and Void* (1970).

The differences between the Gap Theory and the traditional view of a comparatively recent creation of the earth within six literal days are quite profound. In the *first* place, the Gap Theory must redefine the "very good" of Genesis 1:31 ("God saw everything he had made, and, behold, it was very good"), for Adam would have been placed as a very late arrival in a world that had just been destroyed, so that he was literally walking upon a graveyard of billions of creatures (including dinosaurs) over which he would never exercise dominion (Gen. 1:26). Furthermore, this "very good" world would already have become the domain of a fallen and wicked being who is described elsewhere in Scripture as "the god of this world" (II Cor. 4:4).

Secondly, the Gap Theory assumes that carnivorous and other animals were living and dying not only millions of years before Adam, but even before the fall of Satan! But could death have prevailed in the animal kingdom in a sinless world? Does not the Bible indicate that the "groaning and travailing in pain" of the animal kingdom is a result of the Edenic Curse, which came *after* Adam's fall (Rom. 8:20-22)? It was neither nature nor Satan, but *man* who was created to be the king of the earth (Ps. 8, Heb. 2:5-8); and not until *man* deliberately rejected the known will of God did death make its first appearance on this planet (Rom. 5:12) or did animals fall under the "bondage of corruption" (Rom. 8:21). Thus, the Gap Theory seriously compromises the Biblical doctrine of man's original dominion and the doctrine of the Edenic Curse which a holy God inflicted upon the earth because of man's rebellion.

Thirdly, if, according to the Gap Theory, all the animals and plants of the "first world" were destroyed and fossilized, they could have had no genetic relation to the living things of the present world, in spite of the fact that the majority of them appear to be identical in form to modern types. Likewise, those who place human fossils into this "gap" period are forced to the conclusion that such pre-Adamic "men" did not possess an eternal soul (because they obviously died before sin entered the world by Adam).[2]

Fourth, the Gap Theory leaves us with no clear word from God concerning the "original perfect world" (which most advocates of this theory assume to have existed for many millions of years). Thus, we would know *nothing* of the order of events in its creation, the arrangement of its features, or its history (which, we are told, could have constituted 99.9 percent of earth's history thus far); for instead of having the entire first chapter on this important subject, we have only the first verse! Are Christians to assume that before Genesis 1:2 we must look to uniformitarian and evolutionary geologists to fill in the blank? What does this do to Exodus 20:11, which states that *within the six days* (not before the first day), God "made the heavens, the earth, the sea, and all that in them is" (not just plants, animals, and men)?

Finally, the Gap Theory tacitly assumes that Noah's Flood (to which Moses devotes three entire chapters in Genesis) was comparatively insignificant from the standpoint of its geologic and hydrodynamic effects, since all the major fossil-bearing formations were laid down by the supposed Flood of Genesis 1:2 (sometimes referred to as Lucifer's Flood). Obviously, the same fossils were not deposited by two universal floods separated by many centuries! Therefore, the Gap Theory almost requires that No-

---

[2]For recent defenses of the pre-Adamic race view, see Gleason L. Archer, *A Survey of Old Testament Introduction* (Chicago: Moody Press, 1964), pp. 188-189; and Charles F. Baker, *A Dispensational Theology* (Grand Rapids: Grace Bible College Publication, 1971), p. 207.

THE CANADIAN ROCKIES

Mountain ranges in our present world are vastly different from those before the Flood. In the first place, they are as much as *four times* higher in elevation, some being over 28,000 feet above sea level. Such mountains could never have been covered by a global Flood; however, if the earth were completely flat, only 10,000 feet of water would cover it. Secondly, they are packed with billions of fossils of plants and animals that were rapidly buried to great depths by the swirling waters of the great Flood. Mountains before the Flood had *no* fossils, for they were uplifted by God before living things were created (Gen. 1:9-10, 20-22). Thirdly, they are covered with snow and ice. Before the Flood, the great vapor canopy (Gen. 1:6-8) produced a greenhouse effect, trapping the reflection of solar heat (as on Venus today) and providing a warm climate even in the polar regions. The collapse of this vapor canopy during the early weeks of the Flood (Gen. 7:11-12) took the form of snow and ice in the higher latitudes, causing huge glaciers, the sudden freezing of mammoths and other creatures, and the locking up of enough water in the form of ice to expose land bridges from Asia to Alaska and Australia. This intense, but comparatively brief, "ice-age" following the Flood has been considerably modified in recent millennia, causing ocean levels to rise and many sea-mounts and land bridges to be drowned. See Morris, Boardman, and Koontz, *Science and Creation: A Handbook for Teachers* (Creation-Science Research Center, 1971, 2716 Madison Ave., San Diego, Calif. 92116), pp. 52ff.

ah's Flood be localized in its extent and effect in order to give full emphasis to a pre-Adamic catastrophe (cf. Whitcomb and Morris, *The Genesis Flood,* 1961, pp. 5-6). It is futile to argue that the Apostle Peter was referring to a catastrophe in Genesis 1:2 when he wrote that "the world that then was, being overflowed with water, perished" (II Peter 3:6), for he had just referred to Noah's Flood (II Peter 2:5) and would hardly be expected to refer to a different flood without explanation, especially since the only Flood the Lord Jesus Christ ever spoke of was Noah's Flood (cf. Matt. 24:37-39; Luke 17:27)!

Obviously, then, the Gap Theory is not simply a minor deviation from the traditional interpretation of the Genesis creation account. For this reason, the Biblical evidences that have been set forth in its defense need to be carefully examined. Probably the four most significant arguments in support of the Gap Theory are these: (1) The verb translated "was" in Genesis 1:2 (Hebrew: *hayetha*) should better be translated "became" or "had become," thus permitting the idea of a profound change in the earth's condition. (2) The phrase *waste and void* (Hebrew: *tohu wa-bohu*) appears elsewhere only in Isaiah 34:11 and Jeremiah 4:23, and the context of those passages speaks clearly of judgment and destruction. Furthermore, the word *tohu* by itself frequently has an evil connotation. (3) It is highly improbable that God, the author of light, would have originally created the world in darkness, which is generally used in Scripture as a symbol of evil. (4) There seems to be a definite distinction in the first chapter of Genesis between "created" and "made," thus permitting us to assume that many of the things mentioned throughout Genesis 1 were simply re-created.

"Was" or "Became"?

The first supporting argument for the Gap Theory (and the one which Arthur Custance considers crucial) is that the Hebrew verb *hayetha* in Genesis 1:2 should be translated "became" or "had become," thus implying a tremendous transition from perfection to judgment and destruction.

The answer to this argument is that while the verb *hayetha* generally calls for the idea of "become," the word order and sentence structure in Genesis 1:2 (and in a number of other passages) does not permit this translation. If it *had* to be translated "become," then we would *have* to say that Adam and Eve "became" naked (Gen. 2:25), and that the serpent "became" more subtle than any beast of the field (Gen. 3:1)!

Dr. Charles Smith of Grace Theological Seminary has pointed out that the word order in Genesis 1:2 (subject then verb) is most often employed to signal the addition of circumstantial information and the absence of sequential or chronological development, and that is why the Septuagint translators rendered the verb "was" and not "became." Furthermore, he points out that the Hebrew word *waw* which begins Genesis 1:2 is a "circumstantial *waw*" because it is attached to the subject ("the earth") rather than to the verb. Thus, it should properly be translated "now," and the Septuagint translators, who were extremely careful in their handling of the Pentateuch, gave it this translation (*de*).[3]

Very illuminating parallels to the construction in Genesis 1:2 are found in Zechariah 3:1-3 ("he showed me Joshua . . . *Now* Joshua was clothed with filthy garments") and Jonah 3:3 ("Jonah arose, and went into Nineveh . . . *Now* Nineveh was an exceeding great city"). Obviously,

---

[3]Charles R. Smith, in a review of Arthur C. Custance, *Without Form and Void,* the September 1971 issue of *Creation Research Society Quarterly* (2717 Cranbrook Road, Ann Arbor, Mich. 48104). In a published debate on the Gap Theory ("And the Earth Was Without Form and Void," *Journal of the Transactions of the Victoria Institute,* Vol. 78, 1946, pp. 21-23), F. F. Bruce pointed out that if Genesis 1:2 indicated an event subsequent to the creation of verse 1, we might have expected in verse 2 a *"waw* consecutive" with the imperfect tense (i.e., *wattehi ha-arets* instead of *wa-ha-arets hayetha*).

Joshua did not become clothed with filthy garments *after* Zechariah saw him; nor did Nineveh become a great city *after* Jonah entered it! Thus, all the important English translations of Genesis 1:2 are correct in avoiding the idea of "became," because the verse is simply describing the earth's condition just after it was created. In the light of this context and word order, the following theological monstrosity would be produced in Genesis 1:2 if one were to insist on the idea of change or transition in the verb *hayetha*: "Now at the time when God created, the earth had become [already, prior to its creation] unformed and uninhabited"!

"Empty" or "Chaotic"?

This brings us to the second important argument in support of the Gap Theory. If Genesis 1:2 describes the earth's condition at the time of creation, how do we explain the phrase *waste and void* (*tohu wa-bohu*)? Would an infinitely wise and powerful God have created the earth in such a chaotic condition? The only other places in the Bible where the two words *tohu* and *bohu* appear together (Isa. 34:11 and Jer. 4:23) are passages that speak of divine judgment upon Gentile nations and upon Israel. Does not this indicate that these words must refer to judgment and destruction in Genesis 1:2? Even the word *tohu* (translated "without form" in the KJV and "waste" in the ASV), in the twenty verses where it appears without *bohu* in the Old Testament, is sometimes used in an evil sense.

This is admittedly an impressive argument, for one of the most dependable ways to determine the meaning of Hebrew words and phrases is to compare their usage in other passages. Thus, if *tohu* always refers to something evil when used elsewhere in the Old Testament, it would probably have this connotation in Genesis 1:2. But a careful examination of the usage of this word does not support such a meaning. For example, in Job 26:7 we read that God "stretcheth out the north over empty space [*tohu*], and hangeth the earth upon nothing" (ASV). Certainly we are not to find in this verse any suggestion that outer space is basically evil! In some passages the word refers to the wilderness or desert, which is conspicuous for the absence of life (Deut. 32:10; Job 6:18; 12: 24; Ps. 107:40). In most of the places where the word appears in Isaiah, it is paralleled with such words as *nothing* and *nought*.

Of particular interest in this connection is Isaiah 45: 18, which has been used as an important proof text for the Gap Theory. The verse tells us of "the God that formed the earth and made it, that established it and created it not a waste (*tohu*), that formed it to be inhabited." It has been claimed that the *tohu* condition of the earth in Genesis 1:2 could not have been its original condition, because Isaiah 45:18 says it was *not* created a *tohu*. Consequently, God must have originally created an earth replete with living things, and later destroyed it, causing it to *become tohu*.

However, such an interpretation overlooks the true significance of the final phrase in this verse: "formed it to be inhabited." The real point of the passage seems to be that God did not ultimately intend that the world should be devoid of life, but rather that it should be filled with living things. Thus, He did not allow it to *remain* in the empty and formless condition in which He first created it, but in six creative days filled it with living things and fashioned it to be a beautiful home for man. The verse thus speaks of God's *ultimate purpose* in creation, and the contrast in this verse between *tohu* and *inhabited* shows clearly that *tohu* means "empty" or "uninhabited, rather than "judged," "destroyed," or "chaotic." Arthur Custance frankly confesses that "Isaiah 45:18 is a strong witness only to those who already accept the alternative rendering of Gen. 1:2" (*Without Form and Void,* p. 115), especially because the word *tohu* appears again in the following verse (Isa. 45:19) and can hardly be translated "ruin" in that context.

To be sure, the only passages besides Genesis 1:2 where *tohu* and *bohu* appear together — Isaiah 34:11 and Jeremiah 4:23 — are placed in contexts which emphasize divine judgment. But even here the basic meaning of *empty* or *uninhabited* fits well. Since God's ultimate purpose for the earth, and particularly the Holy Land, was that it might be *filled with people* (Isa. 45:18, 49:19-20; Zech. 8:5), it would be a clear evidence of His wrath and displeasure for the promised land to become *empty* and *uninhabited* again. The concept of emptiness, therefore, implies divine judgment only when it speaks of the removal of something that is good. On the other hand, when emptiness follows something that is evil it can be a comparative blessing! An example of this may be found in Christ's work of casting demons out of people (Luke 8:35; cf. Matt. 12:44 — "empty, swept, and garnished").

In spite of the fact that the phrase *tohu wa-bohu* appears elsewhere in judgment contexts and thus takes on an evil connotation in those passages, the same phrase may have a very different connotation when it appears in a different context. Even advocates of the Gap Theory admit that a context of divine judgment seems to be missing in the opening verses of Genesis.[4] It is true that the earth was *empty* as far as living things are concerned, and it was devoid of many of the interesting features it later possessed, such as continents, mountains, rivers, and seas; but it was certainly not chaotic, ruined, or judged. Edward J. Young feels that "it would probably be wise to abandon the term 'chaos' as a designation of the conditions set forth in verse two. The three-fold statement of circumstances in itself seems to imply order. The material of which this earth consists was at that time covered with

---

[4]J. H. Kurtz, *Manual of Sacred History,* 1888, p. xxvi. Cited by Curtis C. Mitchell, "A Biblical and Theological Study of the Gap Theory" (unpublished Th.M. thesis for Talbot Theological Seminary, La Mirada, Calif., 1962), p. 45.

water, and darkness was all about. Over the waters, however, brooded God's Spirit."[5]

So far from being chaotic, the earth *at this particular stage* of creation week can be described as *perfect!* There was nothing wrong with any of the material elements that God brought into existence. The earth had a core, mantle, and crust composed of perfect metal and rock; it was covered with oceans of perfect water; and it was surrounded by a blanket of perfect atmosphere! But it was not yet *complete* as far as God's ultimate purposes were concerned. Likewise, Adam, as a man, was *perfect* when he was first created. But he was "alone" and to this extent *incomplete* until God created Eve to be his companion. For this reason, God could describe Adam's pre-Eve condition as "not good" (Gen. 2:18). In other words, until the creation week ended, Adam himself was *tohu wa-bohu* (perfect at this stage of creation, but alone, incomplete, and thus *comparatively speaking* "not good").

Was the Darkness Evil?

The third major argument used in support of the Gap Theory concerns the darkness of Genesis 1:2. Since darkness is almost always used as a symbol of sin and judgment in the Scriptures (John 3:19; Jude 13, etc.), and since God did not say that the darkness was "good" (as He did concerning the light — Gen. 1:4), proponents of the Gap Theory insist that God originally created the world in light (Ps. 104:2; I Tim. 6:16) and only later plunged it into darkness because of the sin of angels and Satan.

---

[5]Edward J. Young, *Studies in Genesis One* (Nutley, N.J.: Presbyterian and Reformed Pub. Co., 1964), p. 13. Thus, we have an important alternative to the only two interpretations of Genesis 1:2 suggested in the *New Scofield Reference Bible* (p. 1, note #5). In addition to the "Original Chaos" and "Divine Judgment" interpretations suggested there, we have what must be considered the traditional Jewish and Christian interpretation, namely, the "Originally Perfect Yet Incomplete" view.

This, again, is an impressive argument. But *all* of the Biblical evidences need to be taken into consideration. Psalm 104:19-24, for example, makes it quite clear that *physical* darkness (absence of visible light) is not to be considered as inherently evil or as the effect of divine judgment. Speaking of the wonders of the day-night cycle, the Psalmist states: "The sun knowest his going down. *Thou makest darkness,* and it is night, wherein all the beasts of the forest creep forth. The young lions roar after their prey, and seek their food from God. . . . O Jehovah, how manifold are thy works! In wisdom hast thou made them all: the earth is full of thy riches." If the making of darkness is a revelation of God's wisdom and riches, how can it be inherently evil?

In discussing the opening verses of Genesis, Dr. Young points out the true significance of the term *darkness*: "God gives a name to the darkness, just as he does to the light. Both are therefore good and well-pleasing to him; both are created, although the express creation of the darkness, as of other objects in verse two, is not stated, and both serve his purpose of forming the day. . . . Darkness is recognized in this chapter as a positive good for man. . . . Whatever be the precise connotation of the [evening] of each day, it certainly included darkness, and that darkness was for man's good. At times, therefore, darkness may typify evil and death; at other times it is to be looked upon as a positive blessing."[6]

It would seem reasonable to assume that the reason why God did not "see that the darkness was good" is that darkness is not a specific entity, or a thing, but it is rather an absence of something, namely, light. Perhaps it is for this same reason that God did not see that the "firmament" (expanse) of the second creative day was good. It, too, was a rather negative entity, being the empty space between the upper and lower waters. The fact that the absence of light is not incompatible with the presence and

---

[6]Ibid., pp. 21, 35.

blessing of God is evidenced by the statement that "the Spirit of God moved upon the face of the waters" in the midst of this primeval darkness. In the words of the Psalmist, "Even the darkness hideth not from thee, but the night shineth as the day; the darkness and the light are both alike to thee" (Ps. 139:12).

How Many Creative Acts in Genesis 1?

The fourth major supporting argument for the Gap Theory is built upon a supposed distinction between the verbs *created* (*bara*) and *made* (*'asah*). If this distinction is not clearly maintained, then the Gap Theory must collapse, for Exodus 20:11 states that "in six days the Lord made heaven and earth, the sea, and all that in them is." Obviously, if God made (created) *everything* within six days, there would be no room for a long time interval between the creating of the heavens and earth (Gen. 1:1) and the creating of all the other things (Gen. 1:2-31). Therefore the Gap Theory requires that *made* (*'asah*) in Exodus 20:11 should be understood as referring only to the "refashioning" of the heavens and earth in six days after the judgment of Genesis 1:2.

We are disappointed to find the outstanding *New Scofield Reference Bible* (1967) supporting this distinction between *created* and *made* in Genesis 1 — "Only three creative acts of God are recorded in this chapter: (1) the heavens and the earth, v. 1; (2) animal life, vv. 20-21; and (3) human life, vv. 26-27. The first creative act refers to the dateless past" (p. 1, note #4). With regard to Genesis 1:3 ("And God said, Let there be light: and there was light"), the *New Scofield Reference Bible* states that "neither here nor in vv. 14-18 is an original creative act implied. A different word is used. The sense is *made to appear, made visible*. The sun and moon were created 'in the beginning.' The light came from the sun, of course, but the vapor diffused the light. Later the sun appeared in an unclouded sky" (p. 1, note #6).

But this interpretation raises serious questions. In the first place, if God had intended to convey to us the idea that the heavenly bodies (sun, moon, and stars) were already in existence on the first day, but only "appeared" on the fourth day (by a removal of clouds), the verb *to appear* could easily have been used, as in Genesis 1:9 ("and let the dry land appear"). Furthermore, if the sun was created in Genesis 1:1, how could the earth have been shrouded in total darkness in 1:2? No cloud canopy could have excluded the sun's light, for water vapors were not elevated above the firmament until the *second* day of creation.

Even more serious for the Gap Theory is the fact that Genesis 1:21 states that "God created [*bara*] the great sea-monsters. . . ." while verse 25 states that "God made ['*asah*] the beasts of the earth. . . ." Surely we are not to think that sea creatures were directly *created* on the fifth day, but land animals were merely "appointed" or "made to appear" on the sixth day! All those who hold that *bara* and '*asah* cannot be used of the same kind of divine activity are faced with a serious difficulty here. In fact, the difficulty is so severe that the *New Scofield Reference Bible,* in support of this distinction, suggests that the beasts which were *made* on the sixth day (vs. 25) were actually already *created* on the fifth day (p. 2, note #2)! But such an interpretation is impossible since the beasts were obviously brought into existence for the first time on the sixth day ("let the earth *bring forth*," vs. 24). This bringing into existence is described as a work wherein God "*made* the beast of the earth" (vs. 25).

And what does the Gap Theory do about the plant kingdom, which was "brought forth" from the earth on the third day (vss. 11-12)? It must reject the idea that it was created on that day! "It is by no means necessary to suppose that the life-germ of seeds perished in the catastrophic judgment which overthrew the primitive order. With the restoration of dry land and light the earth would 'bring forth' as described" ("Old" *Scofield Reference Bi-*

ble, p. 4, note #3). But this is a very bizarre concept, especially when we realize how rich is God's use of synonyms for "created" in these passages. For example, He commanded the waters to *"swarm* with swarms of living creatures" (vs. 20, ASV). This is explained in the following verse to mean that "God created [*bara*] . . . every living creature that moveth, wherewith the waters swarmed." Likewise, Genesis 2:7 tells us that "God formed [*yatzar*] man of the dust of the ground," which must mean "created," in the light of Genesis 1:27.

Arthur Custance, in his recent book, *Without Form and Void,* even attempts to draw a distinction between God's *making* us in His image and likeness (1:26) and *creating* us in His image (1:27)! Appealing to Origen (third century A.D.), he concludes that "while both image and likeness were *appointed* (*'asah*), only the image itself was *created* (*bara*) by God, the achievement of the likeness being left as something to be wrought out by experience" (p. 180). Thus, according to Dr. Custance, we were not created in the image *and* likeness of God! But if this be true, then God could hardly have *made* man in His *likeness* in the same day He *created* him (Gen. 5:1). Also, we wonder how Adam could have begotten Seth "in his own likeness" as well as "after his image" (5:3).

These examples should suffice to show the absurdities to which we are driven by making distinctions which God never intended to make. For the sake of variety and fullness of expression (a basic and extremely helpful characteristic of Hebrew literature), different verbs are used to convey the concept of supernatural creation. It is particularly clear that whatever shade of meaning the rather flexible verb *made* (*'asah*) may bear in other contexts of the Old Testament, in the context of *Genesis 1* it stands as a synonym for *created* (*bara*). Thus, not only animal life and human life, but also plant life and the astronomic bodies were directly created by God in their appropriate days; and this fact, in the light of Exodus 20:11, is utterly devastating to the Gap Theory.

Other Arguments

In addition to the four major arguments for the Gap Theory discussed above, one frequently hears the claim that the phrase *replenish the earth* in Genesis 1:28 implies that the earth was once filled but now had to be filled *again* (replenished, or refilled). But the verb in the Hebrew text (*maleh*) simply means "to fill," with no suggestion of a repetition. This has been acknowledged by Custance (*Without Form and Void,* p. 8).

Some writers claim that Hebrews 4:3 should be translated "The works were finished from the *downfall* of the world," linking this with the catastrophic interpretation of Genesis 1:2. But this cannot be supported by context or usage of the word (cf. Heb. 9:26). See F. F. Bruce, *The Epistle to the Hebrews* (Eerdmans, 1964), p. 71.

It is also frequently claimed that Ezekiel 28:13-14 demands an originally glorious world before the "waste and void" of Genesis 1:2, for it speaks of Satan as dwelling in "Eden, the garden of God . . . the holy mountain of God" and walking "up and down in the midst of the stones of fire" before his rebellion against God. But it seems clear from a comparison with Daniel 2:45 and Isaiah 14:13 that "the holy mountain of God" must refer to the third heaven of God's immediate presence and not to an earthly domain. It should be noted that Satan was "cast . . . out of the mountain of God . . . *to the ground*" (Ezek. 28:16-17; cf. Isa. 14:12). Apparently the Lord Jesus Christ spoke of this event when He said: "I beheld Satan *fallen* as lightning *from heaven*" (Luke 10:18). It should also be noted that "Eden, the garden of God" was not a garden with trees, flowers, and streams. It was composed of precious stones and "stones of fire" (Ezek. 28:13, 14, 16). When we compare this with the description of the Holy City of Revelation 21:10-21, with its various precious stones, we must conclude that Ezekiel's "garden of God" refers not to an earthly Eden back in Genesis 1:1, but to a heavenly one, from which Satan was cast down to the earth. When

God created the "heavens" at the beginning of the first day of creation week, He apparently created all the angelic beings (including the unfallen Satan), who were thus on hand to sing together and shout for joy at the creation of the earth (Job 38:7). Sometime after creation week and before the temptation of Eve, Satan rebelled against his Creator. The visible earthly effect of his fall would thus not have been a catastrophe in Genesis 1:2, but the Edenic Curse of Genesis 3, which God inflicted upon the entire earth because Adam and Eve, to whom God had given full dominion of the earth, chose to believe and obey Satan rather than God (Rom. 8:20-23).

Conclusion

The Gap Theory continues to claim wide support in the evangelical Christian community because it offers rather impressive Biblical support for a position that does not radically challenge the geologic timetable of modern historical geology. Nevertheless, this theory, on closer inspection, compromises the unity and completeness of the creation account, the original perfection of the world, the genetic continuity of fossil and living forms, the totality of Adam's dominion, and the uniqueness of both the Edenic Curse and the global catastrophism of Noah's Flood.

We would agree with advocates of the Gap Theory that "the earth has undergone a cataclysmic change as a result of divine judgment. The face of the earth bears everywhere the marks of such a catastrophe" ("Old" *Scofield Reference Bible,* p. 3, note #3). However, we would identify this catastrophe with the universal Flood of Noah, which not only occupies three entire chapters of Genesis, but also is referred to by David (Ps. 29:10), Isaiah (54: 9), Christ (Matt. 24:39; Luke 17:27), and Peter (I Peter 3:20; II Peter 2:5; 3:6). It was through the vast and complex current patterns of this year-long Deluge that the living creatures of the entire world were buried and fossil-

THE DINOSAUR

The dinosaurs ("terrible lizards") flourished especially during the period from Adam to the Flood because of the warm and humid climate that characterized the entire pre-Flood world. They did not become extinct *before* Adam, for he was given dominion over *all* the kinds of animals (Gen. 1:28). This has been confirmed by the remarkable discovery of human footprints in the same rock layers with the footprints of dinosaurs (cf. Whitcomb and Morris, *The Genesis Flood,* Presbyterian and Reformed Publishing Co., 1961, pp. 172-176). In the broader sense of the term *dinosaur,* we may say that they are not yet extinct. On the island of Komodo in Indonesia, about a thousand huge dragon lizards still survive, some of them attaining a length of ten feet and a weight of over three hundred pounds *(National Geographic Magazine,* Dec., 1968). And surely the twenty-foot crocodile would qualify as a "terrible lizard"! Since reptiles attain sexual maturity long before their full growth is reached, we need not assume that huge and therefore old individuals represented their kind on Noah's ark. After the Flood, reptilian dinosaurs found themselves confined to a comparatively narrow belt near the equator, and thus in most cases became extinct during the subsequent centuries of desperate struggle for existence against the more versatile and adaptable mammals.

ized in enormous sedimentary strata that underlie every continent of the globe.[7] It is *this* catastrophe that provides for us the God-given answer to the false uniformitarianism of these last days (II Peter 3:4) and thus effectively foreshadows the final destruction of all things by fire at the climax of the Day of the Lord (II Peter 3:7-13).

---

[7]For the hydrodynamic and geologic implications of the Biblical doctrine of the Flood, see John C. Whitcomb, Jr. and Henry M. Morris, *The Genesis Flood* (Nutley, N.J.: Presbyterian and Reformed Pub. Co., 1961); and N. A. Rupke, "Prolegomena to a Study of Cataclysmal Sedimentation," in *Why Not Creation?* ed. Walter Lammerts (Nutley, N.J.: Presbyterian and Reformed Pub. Co., 1970), pp. 141-179. For a recent study of Biblical catastrophism and a critique of the Gap Theory, see Henry Morris, *Biblical Cosmology and Modern Science* (Grand Rapids: Baker Book House, 1970), pp. 62-65.

summary

In total harmony with the methods He employed in bringing highly complex "end products" into existence suddenly during His brief public ministry on the earth, the Son of God created the earth as a dynamic, functioning, fully equipped home for man in a fantastically short period of time. The earth did not evolve from a "chaos" of gas and dust. Neither did it cool down from a molten mass of rock and metal. It was created by purely supernatural means during six literal days and completely furnished with all the basic kinds of living things that have ever existed, including man.

Naturalistic alternatives to the God-revealed account of origins have become increasingly untenable in recent decades as our supply of knowledge in the earth and life sciences has reached staggering proportions. *Astronomers,* with all their amazing discoveries, have still failed to explain how the earth, the sun, the moon, and the stars could have evolved into their present form by natural processes. *Geologists* and *paleontologists* have failed to explain how the huge fossil strata were laid down, how mountains arose from the sea, why dinosaurs became extinct, why all the "missing links" have disappeared, how the ice age began, and how enormous lava flows were poured out upon the earth. *Biologists* and *geneticists* have failed to explain how life could have arisen spontaneously, how the DNA code was formed, why all living creatures reproduce after their kinds, and how the evolutionary hypothesis can survive the deadly formulas of the second law of thermodynamics. *Anthropologists* have conspicuously failed to bridge the yawning bio-cultural chasm that separates the lowest man from the highest animal.

The Bible makes it clear that the early earth was an uncontaminated, highly ordered, and completely harmonious environment for the first human beings. Nature was in harmony with man because man was in harmony with his God. At first, no animals were carnivorous. It is true that plants and fruits were eaten and thus destroyed; and bacteria caused dead vegetable matter to decay; but no animal or human blood was shed through mutual destruction and no natural catastrophes imperiled living things. Although the second law (entropy) was in operation, its harmful effects upon man's world were overbalanced by God's gracious control of all physical and biological systems. Similarly, overpopulation was no threat to the biosphere because God was over, not under, His own laws (and this is still true today!). Reproductive rates in all living things were under His direction.

All of this is, of course, impossible for the mind of man to grasp today through empirical science alone, apart from divine revelation. We are so immersed in a world that "groans and travails in pain" (Rom. 8:22) because of the Edenic Curse (Gen. 3:16-19), that we cannot imagine what the originally perfect earth was like apart from God's explanations in the pages of His written Word. Trapped in the pincers of the first and second laws of thermodynamics, and boxed within an apparently eternal uniformitarian system, we cannot really picture a genuine creation of things, or a sudden reprogramming of living things to "the bondage of corruption," or a supernaturally induced destruction and mass burial of things on a global scale.

But this is basically *our* problem, not God's. He has not only provided for us fascinating and adequate hints of these primeval realities in nature itself, but has also given us a clear and self-authenticating account of His great acts of creation and judgment in the Holy Bible. Many there are, to be sure, who would insist that a comparatively recent earth would be a deception on the part of God. Such accusations are both blasphemous and unfair. If God has *told* us of His creative methods, the order of events in the creation of various entities, and the amount of time which elapsed between these creative acts, we have no one to blame but ourselves for our ignorance. Furthermore, if men were really fair-minded in such matters, they would look at the other side of the ledger of empirical facts which not only permits but *demands* a recent origin of physical and biological systems.

Christians are deeply committed to the proposition that in every problem area, whether it be ultimate origins, ultimate destiny, or ultimate meanings and values and priorities, the God who has revealed Himself supremely in the Lord Jesus Christ and His written Word, cannot lie and cannot finally disappoint those who put their full trust in Him. The natural order *does* demand a Creator; and the wonder of all wonders is that this great Creator also came to earth to pay the full price of human sin and to make it possible for those who believe in Him to experience the fulness of His eternal purpose in creation. With all of its perfections, the Early Earth was therefore only a foretaste of the New Earth which God will some day create (Rev. 21:1).

index
of names and subjects

index
of scripture

bibliography

Archer, Gleason L. *A Survey of Old Testament Introduction.* Chicago: Moody Press, 1964.

Berkouwer, G. C. *The Providence of God.* Grand Rapids: Eerdmans Pub. Co., 1952.

Carnell, Edward John. "Beware of the 'New Deism.'" *His,* 12:3 (December, 1951), 14ff.

Clark, R. T., and Bales, J. D. *Why Scientists Accept Evolution.* Nutley, N.J.: Presbyterian and Reformed Pub. Co., 1966.

Clark, Robert E. D. *Darwin: Before and After.* Chicago: Moody Press, 1967.

Custance, Arthur. *Without Form and Void.* Brockville, Ontario: By the Author, Box 291, 1970.

Davidheiser, Bolton. *Evolution and Christian Faith.* Nutley, N.J.: Presbyterian and Reformed Pub. Co., 1969.

Dixon, Malcolm, and Webb, Edwin. *Enzymes.* 2nd ed. New York: Academic Press, 1964.

Duyvené de Wit, J. J. *A New Critique of the Transformist Principle in Evolutionary Biology.* Kampen, Netherlands: Kok, 1965.

Harris, R. Laird. "The Bible and Cosmology." *Bulletin of the Evangelical Theological Society,* 5:1 (March, 1962), 11-17.

Hooykaas, R. *The Principle of Uniformity.* Leiden: E. J. Brill, 1963.

Kerkut, G. A. *Implications of Evolution.* New York: Pergamon Press, 1960.

Klotz, John W. *Genes, Genesis, and Evolution.* St. Louis: Concordia Pub. House, 1955.

Lammerts, Walter E., ed. *Why Not Creation?* Nutley, N.J.: Presbyterian and Reformed Pub. Co., 1970.

Layzer, David. "Cosmogony." *McGraw-Hill Encyclopedia of Science and Technology.* New York: McGraw-Hill, 1960. Vol. III.

Leith, Thomas H. "Some Logical Problems with the Thesis of Apparent Age." *Journal of the American Scientific Affiliation,* 17:4 (December, 1965), 118-22.

Mixter, Russell, ed. *Evolution and Christian Thought Today.* Grand Rapids: Eerdmans Pub. Co., 1959.

Moorehead, Paul S., ed. *Mathematical Challenges to the Neo-Darwinian Interpretation of Evolution.* Philadelphia: The Wistar Institute Press, 1967.

Mora, Peter T. "The Folly of Probability." *The Origins of Pre-biological Systems.* Edited by S. W. Fox. New York: Academic Press, 1965.

Morris, Henry M. *Biblical Cosmology and Modern Science.* Nutley, N.J.: Craig Press, 1970.

Payne, J. Barton. "The Concept of 'Kinds' in Scripture." *Journal of the American Scientific Affiliation,* 10:2 (June, 1958), 17-19.

Ramm, Bernard. *The Christian View of Science and Scripture.* Grand Rapids: Eerdmans Pub. Co., 1954.

Slusher, Harold S. "Some Astronomical Evidences for a Youthful Solar System." *Creation Research Society Quarterly,* 8:1 (June, 1971), 55-57.

Smart, W. M. *The Origin of the Earth.* Rev. ed. Baltimore: Penguin Books, 1959.

Ulbricht, R. L. V. "Did Life Evolve?" *Chemistry and Industry,* January 8, 1966.

Verduin, Leonard. "Man, a Created Being: What of an Animal Ancestry?" *Christianity Today,* 9:17 (May 21, 1965), 9-15.

Whitcomb, John C., Jr. *The Origin of the Solar System.* Nutley, N.J.: Presbyterian and Reformed Pub. Co., 1964.

Whitcomb, John C., Jr., and Morris, Henry M. *The Genesis Flood.* Nutley, N.J.: Presbyterian and Reformed Pub. Co., 1961.

Young, Edward J. *Studies in Genesis One.* Nutley, N.J.: Presbyterian and Reformed Pub. Co., 1964.

Zimmerman, Paul, ed. *Darwin, Evolution, and Creation.* St. Louis: Concordia Pub. House, 1959.

―――. "Some Observations on Current Cosmological Theories." *Concordia Theological Monthly,* July, 1953.